THE SETTLEMENTS OF THE CELTIC SAINTS IN WALES

The Church and Holy Well of St. Celynin, Caernarvonshire.

THE SETTLEMENTS
OF THE CELTIC SAINTS
IN WALES

BY

E. G. BOWEN, M.A., F.S.A.

Gregynog Professor of Geography and Anthropology
University College of Wales, Aberystwyth

CARDIFF
UNIVERSITY OF WALES PRESS
1956

First Edition 1954
Second Edition 1956

Printed by Hugh Evans and Sons Ltd.,
9 Hackins Hey, and 350-360 Stanley Road, Liverpool

CONTENTS

LIST OF ILLUSTRATIONS

The distribution maps which form the bulk of the illustrations in the first part of this work mark as accurately as possible the position of churches and find-sites but do not name them. In this way the respective distribution patterns (on which so much of the argument depends) are not overshadowed by a mass of place names.

In the map titles as in the text an exception to the general rule stated in the Preface is made in the case of the name of the Patron Saint. Most frequently it is given in its English form (St. David) but at other times the Welsh form (Dewi Sant) is used.

PREFACE

This little book attempts to re-interpret the Age of the Saints in Wales. It is generally agreed that the so-called Dark Ages were an important formative period in the life of the Principality and that those who do not possess some knowledge of this remote period are unable fully to appreciate the cultural features that survive in the present landscape. The names of the saints, the sites they established, and the settlements that grew up around their churches are with us to-day, in a land where the veil between Past and Present is, indeed, a very thin one.

It is appropriate, too, that a work of this kind should appear at the present juncture when we know reasonably well the limitations of the literary sources in this field, but have not, as yet, fully appreciated the significance of the new light that is being shed on the Dark Ages in the West by our enormously increased knowledge of prehistoric archaeology during the last thirty years. This knowledge has illuminated the history of Wales over a period of nearly two thousand years before the Age of the Saints, and in this way can act as a bright light against which the proto-historic period can now be silhouetted.

Silhouettes, however, reflect only the major outlines and composition of the scene—they do not provide details of a precise nature. Thus, the reader will fail to find in this book details of the precise year in which a particular saint either was born or died, or, for that matter, anything new concerning his or her family associations or political allegiancies. A broad general picture alone is outlined, and if it differs from that based on the ' Lives ' of the saints, the difference is very largely the measure of the new knowledge revealed.

In the compilation of this story I am greatly indebted to

the works of others and I have tried to give full acknowledgement to them in the footnotes and bibliography. I owe a deep debt of gratitude to scholars such as the late Principal Ifor L. Evans, D.Litt., Professors Sir Ifor Williams, D.Litt., Henry Lewis, D.Litt., T. Jones-Pierce, M.A., H. J. Fleure, F.R.S., together with Sir Cyril Fox, F.B.A., the late Dr. V. E. Nash-Williams and Miss L. F. Chitty, F.S.A. for constant help and inspiration in this work. My colleagues in the Department of Geography and Anthropology—Messrs. Harold Carter, M.A. and J. Gareth Thomas, M.A., together with Mr. Alwyn D. Rees, M.A., Director of Extra-Mural Studies, have read the manuscript and made several useful suggestions which I have adopted.

Place-names in Wales are given throughout in their Welsh form except in those instances where long accustomed usage makes the Anglicized form more suitable in an English text. The Welsh spellings are those approved of by the Board of Celtic Studies of the University of Wales and I am most grateful to Dr. Elwyn Davies, the Secretary of the University Press Board, for his personal help and co-operation in this and many other matters connected with this book. The spellings adopted for the names of saints presented further complications. It was decided that when reference was made to a saint in a Welsh context the Welsh form of his or her name should be used, but if the same saint is mentioned in a Cornish or in an Irish context, the local Cornish or Irish form should be used. Thus St. Petroc of Cornwall would become St. Pedrog in Wales. I gratefully acknowledge the valuable assistance given to me by my colleague Professor Thomas Jones, D.Litt., of the Department of Welsh Language and Literature, in the preparation of this work and in particular for his help with everything related to Welsh orthography.

My thanks are also due to my draughtsman, Mr. Morlais Hughes, for the care which he has taken in the preparation of the maps and diagrams ; to Miss Ethel R. Payne, M.Sc. of the Department of Education, University of Birmingham,

who has prepared the Index and to my sister Miss Mary
E. Bowen, J.P. who has helped greatly with the proof
reading. I should also like to express my appreciation of
the interest, skill and attention given to this work by the
Printers in the course of its publication.

PREFACE TO THE SECOND EDITION

The reprinting of the text in June, 1956 has offered the
opportunity of correcting a number of errors as well as of
revising certain matters relating to the nature of Celtic
dedications, and the linguistic situation in the Celtic Lands
in the immediate post-Roman centuries.
The author wishes to thank the numerous reviewers first
of all for their kindly notices of the book, and still more
for many valuable suggestions, the majority of which have
been incorporated in this edition.

INTRODUCTION

THE widespread occurrence of place names involving the prefix ' Llan ' is a well marked feature of the Welsh landscape. The word originally meant ' an enclosure ' as we find by the compound words ' perllan ' (an orchard), ' gwinllan ' (a vineyard) or ' corlan ' (a sheep fold). This basic meaning of ' a clearing ' or ' an open space ' appears to be kept in the word ' llannerch ' (' a green glade ' originally in forested country) as seen in such place names as Llannerch Aeron in Cardiganshire. In the vast majority of place names in which it occurs it is found in a religious context linked with the name of a Celtic saint[1] as at Llandeilo or Llanddeiniol. In such instances it means land consecrated either to or by the saint named.

On the original sacred enclosure a cell or cells would be built, and in later times they would be replaced by a church or monastery, so that the word ' llan ' at the present time comes to be used in its secondary meaning signifying a church.[2] The urban centres, villages and hamlets that have gathered (in some cases) around the church took

[1] These were Celtic Christian missionaries who have been given the general title of ' saints, although ' monks ' would be a better term. They were active in establishing churches, oratories and monasteries in Western Europe between the 5th and 8th centuries A.D.

[2] There are, however, instances where the prefix is followed by purely locational terms such as Llanuwchllyn in Merionethshire which literally means ' the church at the head of the lake,' or Llandaf, the cathedral church near Cardiff, which signifies ' the church near the river Taf '; sometimes also Llangoed ' the church in the woods.' It should be noted that on some occasions the prefix is followed not by the name of any individual saint but by an indication that the church belonged to a number of saints e.g. there is both a Llanddeusant and a Llanpumsaint (lit. ' the church of the two saints ' and ' the church of the five saints ' respectively) in Carmarthenshire, and a Llantrisant (lit. ' the church of the three saints ') in both Anglesey and Glamorganshire. Sometimes other numbers are recorded in a similar context. See Sir Ifor Williams, *Enwau Lleoedd*, Cyfres Pobun V, (Lerpwl, 1945), pp. 54ff.

their names from the church in question, and in some parts of Wales ' llan ' is used to refer to the present built-up area as a whole and not to the church in particular.[1]

To revert to the churches themselves. Celtic churches bear the names of Saints who are frequently unknown outside the Celtic world. This feature is different from the usual type of dedication found in other churches of Western Christendom. Early Celtic churches were as a rule named after their original founders, or, possibly, after the founder of the monastery to which the saint establishing the community might belong. This is comparable with the primitive Christian custom, as in Rome itself, of naming meeting places for worship after their founders, or the owner of the house (e.g. the *titulus Vestinae*). It is likely that the practice in Celtic Lands was an extension of this idea, thus bringing the Celtic church at the time of its formation in the fifth century into line with the conservative continental practice of the day. Only in later centuries would these designations of the churches become dedications in the normal sense of the term.

Outside Wales the term ' Llan ' is (owing to linguistic differences) less frequently found. It occurs in Cornwall and Brittany, although in the latter country ' Loc ' is more frequently found as a prefix to place-names involving the name of a Celtic saint. Kil—or Cil—is found in a similar context in Ireland and Scotland, while the ' Keills ' of the Isle of Man are well known.

It must be stressed, however, that even in Wales place names with the prefix ' Llan ' do not always contain the name of a *Celtic* saint. Besides examples already cited we must allow for the frequent occurrence of Llanfair (St. Mary's church) and Llanfihangel (St. Michael's church). These and similar examples of the use of the prefix obviously bear no relation to the Celtic Church. The cult of the Archangel became popular in Wales in the 10th and 11th

---

[1] The poet Ceiriog writes ' Fe basiai Gwendolen trwy'r llan ' (Gwendolen passed through the *village*). *Oriau'r Hwyr*, 1860, 28.

centuries, while the dedication or re-dedication of churches
to the Virgin is almost without exception in Wales a feature
of the Norman penetration, or of its influence on the native
Princes. Likewise, it should not be assumed that all
churches dedicated to Celtic saints in Wales have the prefix ' Llan.' While this is by far the most common occurrence, dedications to Celtic saints are sometimes associated
with the word Merthyr, as at Merthyr Tudful in Glamorgan
or Merthyr Cynog in Brecknockshire. Merthyr used in
this respect is equivalent in meaning to ' memorial '—a
memorial to the saint thus named. A few other prefixes
to the names of Celtic saints are found in Welsh place names,
particularly Bod- and Tre- (lit. 'dwelling of' and ' township
of'—respectively), and occasionally Llech-, Maen- and Ty- (lit.
'slate of-', 'stone of-' and 'house of-' respectively). Sometimes,
the settlement retains the saint's name without a prefix of any
kind as in Baglan in Glamorgan or Llywel in Brecknockshire.[1]
Even though there are many instances in the Principality, and
elsewhere in the Celtic lands, of settlements associated with
churches dedicated to Celtic saints with no indication of this
fact surviving in the name by which the settlement is now
known, nevertheless, it would be agreed that a better
knowledge of the various factors, both cultural and physical,
that helped to determine the initial location of Celtic churches
is much to be desired. Such knowledge, indeed, may be
considered a pre-requisite of all who seek to interpret success-
fully the settlement pattern shown on representative topographic sheets of the Celtic lands.

Enough has already been said to show that it is possible
by an examination of place names and local historical
material to list all the known churches and chapels in Wales
which are now, or were in former times, dedicated to Celtic
saints. The list can then be scrutinized carefully to investi-
gate the antiquity of the dedications. In its final form it is
likely to represent those churches and chapels whose sites
were originally associated with a settlement made by the

[1] For full discussion see J. Fisher, ' Welsh Church dedications,' *Trans. Hon.
Soc. Cymmrod.* Vol. 15, 1906-07.

particular itinerant saint whose name they bear. From lists of this kind the geographer can prepare maps to show the distribution of all the known dedications to either an individual saint or a group of saints, thus marking his, her or their 'patria' or 'sphere of influence' in the Dark Ages.[1] Such work, which has not previously been attempted on a comprehensive scale, is able to provide new clues to the interpretation of the proto-historic period in the West.

Hitherto scholars have been almost entirely dependent for their knowledge of this period on the 'Lives' of the various saints which claim to give an account of their work, their travels and their contemporaries. Unfortunately, this seemingly promising source is a most unsatisfactory one from the point of view of the modern student, as these texts are known to have been written many hundreds of years after the particular saint, whose life history they purport to give, was supposed to have lived. Furthermore, they are packed with material relating to the supernatural which, while of interest to the social anthropologist and student of primitive religion is hardly a satisfactory source for the historical geographer. Their value to the modern student is further depreciated by the fact that they were almost all written by medieval monks who were naturally eager to further the interests of their own church and (as far as Wales is concerned) those of the Norman conquerors as well. We know, for example, that the most important collection of the 'Lives' of the Welsh saints is found in a British Museum manuscript now known as Vespasian A XIV which was written in Brecon Priory towards the close of the 12th century.[2] These 'Lives' in the form in which they have come down to us suffer from all the weaknesses noted above. It is possible, of course, and even probable, that the authors had older written material before them

---

[1] In order to increase as much as possible the intensity of the cultural background the material plotted might include holy wells and other sacred sites still bearing the name of the particular saint.

[2] See G. H. Doble, *Saint Paul of Leon*, Cornish Saints' Series No. 46, 1941, p. 25.

which they proceeded to adapt to their special requirements. We are more certain of this because in a few very exceptional instances we possess the ' Life ' of a Celtic saint written down within a relatively short period after his lifetime, and apparently uninfluenced by later medieval theological and ecclesiastical prejudices.[1]

A considerable literature has grown up in an attempt to interpret the ' Lives ' of the Saints. It has been devoted either to the textual or literary criticism of the ' Lives ' themselves, or to an analysis of the historical, pseudo-historical, or marginal material contained within them. Indeed, the publication of the final volume of Baring Gould and Fisher's *Lives of the British Saints* in 1913 was thought to mark the completion of all that was possible in this particular field of study for many generations to come. The work of the Rev. A. W. Wade-Evans[2] and the late Canon Gilbert H. Doble[3] has added considerably to our knowledge of the ' Lives ' of the Welsh and Cornish saints in the forty years that have intervened since 1913, while the enormous developments made in the study of pre-historic, Roman and post-Roman archaeology during this same period have made available a new and very important cultural background to the study of the period. Archaeology has advanced not only as the result of expertly conducted excavations in the field, but also by the intensive study of the geographical distribution of archaeological finds, inscriptions and other elements of material culture belonging to different periods. In this way ancient routeways as well as clearly marked cultural regions are distinguished in pre- and proto-historic Britain.[4] This geo-

[1] The *Vita Samsonis* written by a monk of Dol probably at the beginning of the 7th century and certainly not later than the middle of the 9th century is a well known example. Also Wrdisten's *Vita S. Winwaloei* and Wrmonoc's *Vita Pauli* fall into this category.

[2] A. W. Wade-Evans, *Vitae Sanctorum* (Cardiff, 1944), and other publications.

[3] G. H. Doble, *The Cornish Saints' Series* Nos. 1-48. Also *The Welsh Saints* Nos. 1-5, 1942-1944.

[4] An outstanding example of such a study is Sir Cyril Fox's *Personality of Britain*, Fourth Edition, 1943.

B

graphical aspect of the study can be applied to the Age of
the Saints by studying dedication-distribution patterns of
the type already described. Such patterns can easily be
correlated with maps indicating cultural areas in prehistoric and Roman times. It should be emphasized that
this approach is all the more significant in Wales, or for that
matter, elsewhere in Highland Britain, since one of the
distinguishing features of these lands is the marked continuity of tradition that characterizes their cultural life.
Several suggestive results have already been obtained by
the application of this method in a preliminary way.[1]
It is proposed to adhere to the distributional method in the
first section of this book, because apart from its ability to
shed new light on the problem before us, it has the supreme
advantage of allowing the investigator to be independent
of the unsatisfactory material so frequently preserved in the
' Lives.' Thus, the literary sources for the Age of the Saints
will not be allowed to influence the general argument here
presented, but on the other hand the fullest use will be made
of the topographical allusions in the texts, and stress will be
laid on the way in which saints linked together in the
narratives appear to have dedications close to each other on
the ground. Fundamentally, the aim in Part I of this book
is to explore and expand in the light of recent knowledge,
all that is implicit in the remark of the great Breton scholar
M. Joseph Loth when he wrote ' In Wales, Cornwall and
Brittany, it is not the "Lives" of the saints that tell us most
about the existence of the saints and the national organ-
ization of religion, but the names of places.'[2]

There are, however, a number of initial difficulties en-
countered in developing the distributional studies outlined
above. First of all, there are obvious matters such as the
possibility that there may have been instances of more
than one saint bearing the same name, in which case it
would be quite impossible to distinguish their respective

---

[1] E. G. Bowen, ' The Travels of the Celtic Saints', *Antiquity* XVIII, 1944 and
' The Settlements of the Celtic Saints in South Wales', *Antiquity*, XIX, 1945.

[2] J. Loth, *Les Noms des Saints Bretons*, 1910.

cults from the dedications which have survived. Then, we are not certain to what extent the facts we possess are representative of the actual conditions existing in the Age of the Saints. It is most probable that a very large number of religious communities were established of which we have now no trace or record of any kind.

Another difficult matter is the problem of the genuine antiquity of the sites we know of, and whether we can be certain that they belonged to the Age of the Saints. We have already allowed for the fact that followers of a particular saint might dedicate to their special monastic patrons the churches they established, as, for example, the founder of Abernethy dedicated its church to St. Brigid although there is no evidence that she ever visited Scotland in person. The case of St. Ninian dedicating his church at Whithorn to St. Martin at this early date has been doubted by scholars, for the very valid reason that St. Martin was not a martyr and early dedications were in honour of martyrs only. So this dedication obviously belongs to a later age. There is also the further problem of the projection of dedications to Celtic Saints outside the Age of the Saints proper. This certainly did occur, for we know of a Norseman named Orlyg who built a church in Iceland circa A.D. 900 and dedicated it to St. Columba at the desire of a Bishop Patrick who had taught him in the Hebrides.[1] While this interesting example shows that tenth century Christian Norsemen dedicated their churches, it certainly does not prove that the great St. Columba or one of his immediate followers had visited Iceland. Throughout the Middle Ages there was undoubtedly a revival of the cult of many a Celtic saint and new churches were dedicated to them throughout the Celtic lands. Most frequently a revival of a saint's cult, expressing itself in new dedications, coincided with the publication of his ' Life.' It may be advisable to illustrate this point again from outside Wales. During the 12th century there was a great recrudescence of

[1] T. H. B. Graham, and W. G. Collingwood, ' Patron Saints of the Diocese of Carlisle ', *Trans. Cumb. & West. Ant. & Arch. Soc.* 1925, p. 11.

interest in the sixth century Celtic saint Kentigern (Cyndeyrn) who is the patron of Glasgow cathedral and who had associations with Wales as well.   In the 12th century two biographies or ' Lives ' of Kentigern appeared, the later of the two by Jocelyn of Furness who said that he had found the necessary materials in Ircland.   Before his book was finished the church at Crosthwaite in Cumberland had been built and dedicated to St. Kentigern on the strength of an alleged tradition that he had preached at this place.   It will, however, be noted that in this instance, as well as in almost all known instances of the revival of a saint's cult in the Middle Ages, the new church was placed in territory where not only a tradition of the saint's activity survived, but also where there were several churches previously dedicated to him.[1]   In other words, re-dedication takes place within the original culture area.   While Canon Doble does not deal specifically with this important matter of the revival of a saint's cult in the Middle Ages (which, if it were very extensive would invalidate the premises on which this book rests) his studies do help us very considerably. He has, in all his monographs,[2] stressed the point that it frequently happens that dedications to individual saints associated with one another in the ' Lives ' are often found close to each other in adjoining or nearby parishes.   He draws particular attention to the geographical proximity of the various elements in the story of the life of a saint. This is fundamentally significant for our thesis, for if we wish to assume that all real historical facts concerning a saint had already vanished before his ' Life ' was written down in the Middle Ages, then we can explain such topographical evidence only in one of two ways.   First, we may assume that the dedications are pre-medieval ;   then the ' Life ' could be written in an attempt to explain the dedications of near-by churches.   Alternatively, we could argue that these churches were re-dedicated in the Middle Ages to coincide with the publication of the ' Life ' of a saint.

[1] Ibid, pp. 10-11.
[2] G. H. Doble, op. cit.

In this case, since the area over which a particular saint's cult spread is always too distinctive to be the arbitary creation of the medieval mind, the writer of the ' Life ' must have had in his possession ancient traditions relating to the specific region in which re-culting took place. The evidence of the revival of the cult of St. Kentigern in the twelfth century fits into this background. All arguments, therefore, indicate that a carefully checked dedication-distribution yields a pattern that is certainly pre-medieval and probably survives in most instances directly from the Age of the Saints.

Another serious problem confronting the investigator of early Celtic church dedications (particularly in Wales) is the considerable amount of re-dedication that took place following upon the Norman penetration and the arrival of the medieval religious orders.[1]   Sometimes a Celtic saint's name was added to the patrons of a Norman church, as St. Teilo's was to Llandaf cathedral, in order to bolster up the claims of rival dioceses to various Celtic churches, but most frequently the Roman clergy re-dedicated the original Celtic church to one of their favourite saints, usually St. Mary or St. Peter. These changes which came about in the Middle Ages have greatly limited the number of Celtic dedications now available for study. Sometimes the original Celtic dedication can be recovered from historical references as, for example, at Kilpeck in Herefordshire which was originally dedicated to St. David and is now dedicated to St. Mary, or Rhiwabon parish church in North Wales formerly dedicated to St. Collen but now to St. Mary. At other times the former dedication has survived in a dual dedication as at Llanhamlach in Brecknockshire which is dedicated to St. Illtud and St. Peter, or at Llanfwrog in Denbighshire dedicated to SS. Mwrog and Mary. Occasionally, the dual dedication occurs in the actual name of the church as at Eglwys Fair a Churig (the church of St. Mary and St. Curig) in north-western Carmarthen-

[1] There might have been a certain amount of re-dedication taking place among rival cults even during the Age of the Saints (see p.63).

shire. A geographical distribution of the non-Celtic dedications in Wales would show them to be most thickly distributed in the areas that were most thoroughly Normanized in the Middle Ages.

In spite of the difficulties which prevent us from being able to reconstruct with certainty the complete picture of the settlements of the Celtic saints in Wales, nevertheless, the material used to build up the distribution maps in this work covers a good sample of the whole and probably, too, gives a reasonable indication of the pattern of the complete but unobtainable picture. As long as the dedication-distribution maps are interpreted with care[1] we are confident that they can be taken as indications of the *patria* or sphere of influence of an individual saint, even if they do not imply actual foundations by the saint himself. In this way we are able to delimit a number of culture areas in Wales in the Dark Ages, upon which are based the arguments developed in the first part of this book.

The second part of the work deals with another aspect of the problem and concerns the geographer more particularly. It may be described as a settlement study. We have already noted how the great majority of the cells originally established by the Celtic saints developed into churches and each church in turn became a potential pivot for further settlement. A settlement study should deal with all aspects of the problem ; position, site and form ; and, in order to marshall the data concerned, a card catalogue was prepared of the 614 carefully checked examples of ancient churches either now, or formerly known to be, dedicated to Celtic saints in Wales. Each slip gives the name and dedication of each church, its altitude above sea level, together with details of its site and the extent of settlement gathered around it at the present time. Using the data thus collected the geographer can map the position of the churches, analyse their sites, and classify the settlement patterns. This tripartite approach provides a

---

[1] See Kenneth Jackson's review of W. D. Simpson, *The Celtic Church in Scotland*, *Antiquity* IX, 1935, pp. 492-4.

convenient chapter division for the second part of this book.

It is obvious that the distribution of Celtic churches is dependent on two sets of factors. There are the purely historical and cultural factors associated with the objectives, motives and provenance of the respective saints ; their methods of travel and the routeways frequented in their day. All this is treated in Part I. Secondly, there are the major physical factors. Some, such as accessibility to tidal water clearly favoured by the saints, while others, such as high altitude, steep slopes, bogland and marsh were carefully avoided. These considerations are dealt with in Part II, as they are of major concern to the historical geographer who, however broad his terms of reference may be, cannot neglect the physical aspect.

The study of site involves more detailed considerations. Minor facets of the relief such as valley benches, river terraces, alluvial fans and various superficial geological deposits now assume importance. Material for such detailed studies is not readily available in print. Physiographical field-work in Wales is, as yet, in its infancy and few areas are well documented. Geological maps showing the superficial drift are available for limited areas only in the Principality, so that an analysis of the six hundred sites in question could not be completed from cartographical and printed sources alone, even if this were desirable. Field work was essential, and there are few of the six hundred sites that have not been visited over a period of years. The details of the site on which the church stands were in every case carefully recorded on the card catalogue. Sometimes difficulties of an historical nature arise, in so far that the present church is known to have been moved from its former, and possibly original, site within historic times. Sometimes, this is the result of natural causes as when an ancient Celtic chapel on the sea coast at Dinas, Pembrokeshire, was washed away by the waves and replaced by another on a less exposed site.[1] More frequently, the change of site was determined

[1] Roy. Comm. Anc. Mon. (Wales) VII, *Pembrokeshire*. H.M.S.O. 1925. No. 907.

by man, as in the case of St. David's church at Brechfa, Carmarthenshire which has been moved a few yards further away from the older church in relatively recent times.[1] On some (fortunately rare) occasions a church has been moved from its original site and re-dedicated at the same time. The church of Llansanffraid Deuddwr in Radnorshire (originally dedicated to St. Ffraid (Brigid) as the name indicates) was moved to a new site in 1778 and the dedication changed to to that of St. Winifred.[2] Difficulties of this kind are known to affect less than two per cent of the total number of sites so that the material covered under this heading in the second part of the book may be considered as likely to be fully representative of the original choice of sites in Wales.

Settlement form has long attracted the attention of geographers but frequently they have been content merely to classify the varied patterns directly from the present day topographic maps with little regard for the past. We look upon settlement form not as something given in advance either by nature or culture but as a pattern that has gradually emerged in response to either static or changing geographical values. The patterns of settlement that have gathered around the original Celtic churches well illustrate the significance of this historical approach. They grade from urban nuclei of considerable magnitude, through medium-sized villages into hamlets, and downwards to smaller clusters of some half a dozen farms or houses, too small to attain even hamlet status, while frequently the church is found completely isolated with no settlement nearby, with the possible exception of the vicarage or rectory. No one has yet dealt with the settlements gathered around Celtic churches either from an historical point of view or on a scale covering the Principality as a whole. The settlement around every church has been examined on the 1:25,000 sheets, classified, and noted on the card catalogue ; while the Tithe maps, the original edition of the

---

[1] Ibid. *Carmarthenshire* V. H.M.S.O. 1917, No. 46.
[2] Ibid. *Radnorshire* III. H.M.S.O. p. 103.

Ordnance Survey, and manuscript sources (wherever available) have been consulted in preparing material for the relevant chapter in Part II.

It is hoped that sufficient has now been said to explain the dual approach adopted in this book. It is essential, however, to re-emphasize that this work has no claim to be a new history of the Celtic Church in Wales ; its historical, political, ecclesiastical and literary aspects are kept in the background so that full emphasis can be placed on the study of proto-historic culture areas and the settlement patterns associated with the sites of Celtic churches.

PART I

CHAPTER I

IN THE BEGINNING

N O one knows exactly how, when, or where Christianity first appeared in Wales, so we are presented at the outset with a fertile field for speculation. There were undoubtedly some Christians in the Roman Army of the Occupation, but they could not have been very many. Only in the south-eastern area, where there was a fairly strong Romano-British population, do we find slight evidence of a Christian element in Roman times as witnessed by the tradition of the martyrdom of Saints Aaron and Julius near Caerlleon. The withdrawal of Roman troops from Wales by Magnus Maximus in 383 A.D. ended the effective Roman occupation of the country, although archaeological and numismatic evidence shows that some form of sub-Roman life persisted amidst the ruins in South-eastern Wales for possibly another century or more.[1] It is in this setting that we get definite evidence of Christianity. The small Christian church at Caer-went has its foundations in a debris layer one foot above the ruins of a Roman bath,[2] while recent excavations have shown that the burials discovered in 1888 at a Roman villa near Llanilltud Fawr in south Glamorgan were orientated in the Christian manner in an east-west direction, and that the graves were cut through the mosaic floor of the buildings indicating that we have a Christian cemetery of late 4th century date on the site of a ruined villa and not the massacred remains of the last Romano-British inhabitants.[3] It is tempting to see in these examples of Christianity in a post-Roman context a

[1] Aileen Fox, *A Hundred Years of Welsh Archaeology*, Centenary Volume 1846-1946, Cambrian Archaeological Association, 'Early Christian Period' pp. 106-7.

[2] V. E. Nash-Williams, *Archaeologia* LXXX (1930), p. 235.

[3] V. E. Nash-Williams, *Arch. Camb.* 1938, p. 255.

14

case for its survival into the Dark Ages, especially in an area such as this with strong Romano-British traditions. The arguments could be extended to show that as this surviving Christian community became more and more isolated from the Roman world it began to develop new features of its own, which ultimately blossomed into the Celtic Christianity that flourished so vigorously in these parts, and spread, not only over most of Highland Britain but also into Brittany. Unfortunately, there is little evidence for such a continuity of tradition. It is true that much can be made of the story of St. Tathan or Tatheus, the son of an Irish king, who towards the end of the fifth or the beginning of the sixth century is supposed to have arrived by sea at the Severn mouth and obtained from the local ruler a grant of land at Caer-went whereon he built a collegiate church. Some modern historians have plausibly identified the post-Roman Christian church revealed by archaeology at Caer-went with the church established by St. Tathan. Even if we allow for the identification, the implication of this story is that Celtic Christianity was intruded into these parts by sea from the West and is not a development *in situ* from Romano-British roots. The archaeological evidence, as we have seen, does not support the theory that this church was associated with the Christian community that prevailed in these parts during the occupation. It was clearly built in ' post-Roman ' times, although stylistically it is of the Silchester basilican type. It would be highly improbable that an Irish saint of the late fifth or early sixth century would erect a church of this character even in these strongly Romanized parts. The simplest explanation is that the Christianity found in a post-Roman archaeological context at Caer-went and at Llanilltud Fawr represents the last surviving elements of the Christianity that had existed in Britain in late Imperial days and the architectural affinities of the small church at Caer-went with the Silchester church, strongly suggest that the sea-plain of south-east Wales in immediate post-Roman times received among other refugees some Christian colonies, possibly from the Sil-

chester-Cirencester area which was at this time beginning to
feel the pressure of barbarian raids.[1] Continuity, therefore, is extremely difficult to prove.[2] Any lingering doubts
on this question have been dispelled by Dr. V. E. Nash-
Williams' outstanding work on the Early Christian Monuments of Wales.[3] He has proved conclusively that after
the withdrawal of Roman power Christianity entered
Wales anew and this time unmistakably by the western
sea routes.   Dr. Nash-Williams has been able on epigraphical and other grounds to divide the Early Christian
inscribed stones of Wales into three major categories.
The first group belongs to the 5th and 6th centuries A.D.,
the second group to the 7th and 8th centuries and the third
to the 9th and 10th.   In this chapter we are primarily
concerned with the first group.   The lettering on the stones
in this group is usually in Roman capitals with few ligatures,
but in the later part of the period we have Roman capitals
and half uncials mixed together in the same inscription.
The really important point, however, is that there is
abundant evidence in the style of writing adopted, in the
type of formula employed, and sometimes in the actual
allusions made, not only to date the memorials with some
precision, but also to trace back their cultural origin to the
Lyon and Vienne areas of Gaul.[4] Furthermore, their
distribution is markedly concentrated in the three north-
western and the three south-western counties, suggesting
strongly that the early Christians who are commemorated
on the memorials moved into Wales by sea from Western
Gaul.   They would appear to have utilized what remained

[1] It is even possible as Dr. Nash-Williams recently suggested that the little
church is actually of Byzantine origin.   The small oblong building with an
apse at the east end and a narthex at the west is very similar in plan to early
Eastern churches.   The finding of seven Byzantine coins of the 6th-9th centuries
at Caer-went adds considerable interest to this theory, and certainly shows that
Caer-went in the Dark Ages had at least occasional contacts with the Byzantine
world, presumably at the hands of merchants using the western sea-routes.

[2] We shall return later to the story of St. Tathan.

[3] V. E. Nash-Williams, *The Early Christian Monuments of Wales* (Cardiff,
1950).

[4] V. E. Nash-Williams, op. cit., see inscribed stones No. 33 and No. 104
especially.

of the Roman road system in south Wales to get into the
Brecon region where there is another marked concentration
of these inscriptions (see Fig I). As Dr. Nash-Williams puts
it ' the Western orientation of Wales and its isolation from
Anglo-Saxon England at this period is clearly demonstrated.' His map also demonstrates in no uncertain manner
the complete cultural break with the past. There is a
marked absence of these early Christian memorial stones
in south-eastern Wales and in the Borderland, that is, in the
very areas where Roman life and culture struck its deepest
roots during the period of the occupation, and where there
is known to have been a late survival of Romano-British
Christianity. We have, therefore, to reckon with a new cultural movement involving the spread of Christian immigrants
into Wales from Gaul by way of our western approaches.

Such extensive movements in the western seas at this
time are in no way surprising to the student of prehistoric
archaeology. Sir Cyril Fox[1] has familiarized us with the
concept of the dual character of Britain with its Highland
and Lowland Zones. He has also shown that at periods
when the south-eastern or Lowland zone was in a disturbed
state owing to invasions from the continent, the Highland
zone conversely entered upon a period of intense activity.
Movements of peoples and cultures were witnessed along
the sea-routes that connect its western facing peninsulas
and islands with the continent. The western seaways were
active from the late 1st century B.C. to the mid-1st century
A.D. following upon Caesar's pacification of Gaul and his
raids on south-eastern England and the ultimate Claudian
conquest of the Lowland Zone. During this period Iron
Age peoples had carried advanced techniques of textile and
metal working, corn-grinding and pottery, derived from
south-west British and north-west Gaulish cultures, northwards to the Hebrides and Scapa Flow.[2] Similarly, at

---

[1] Sir Cyril Fox, *The Personality of Britain*, 4th Edit., Cardiff 1943, see also
Sir H. J. Mackinder, *Britain and the British Seas* (Oxford, 1905).
[2] Sir Lindsay Scott, ' Gallo-British Colonies', *Proc. Prehist. Soc.* XIV,
1948, pp. 46-125.

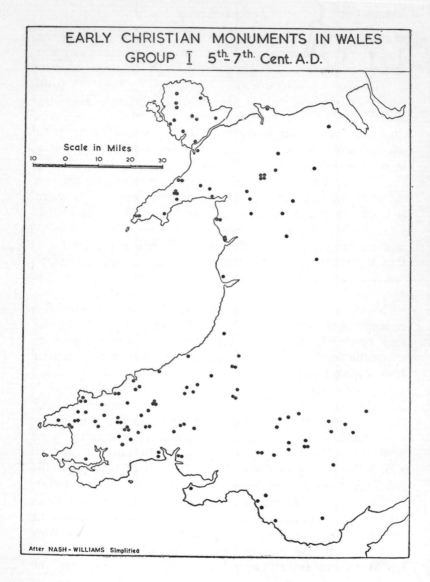

EARLY CHRISTIAN MONUMENTS IN WALES
GROUP Ī 5th-7th Cent. A.D.

Scale in Miles

After NASH-WILLIAMS Simplified

Fig. 1

the close of the Roman occupation, when Imperial power was fading in south-eastern Britain, and these parts were once more exposed to barbarian invasion, activity returned to the western sea-routes. It was along these routes (which alone in the fifth and sixth centuries A.D. were able to maintain contact with what remained of Roman civilization in Gaul and the Western Mediterranean) that Christianity now entered Wales anew from the west.

We have already noted that the Early Christian inscribed stones in Wales have distinct cultural associations with Christian communities in Gaul and we know from other sources that there was at this time a powerful monastic movement within the Gallic church—a movement that can be traced to the monastic establishments at Lerins and on other islands off the Mediterranean shores of France and Italy, and ultimately to the Egyptian desert.[1] Such is the background for the story of St. Martin of Tours, who must be looked upon as one of the founders of Gallic monasticism in the form that it spread into Highland Britain, because it is certain that it was a Christianity with a strong ' monastic ' or ' eremetical ' flavour that these Gallic *peregrini* brought with them into Western Britain at this time.[2] Before leaving this discussion on the significance of the western sea-routes and the re-introduction of Christianity into Wales, mention must be made of the fact that movements from Gaul were not the only ones taking place in the western seas at this period. There is archaeological evidence to show that following the withdrawal of Roman control from Britain many Irish immigrants crossed the Irish sea and settled in the Highland Zone. Their influence is particularly well marked in south-west Wales. Some of them brought with them, (possibly at the beginning of the fifth century) a special form of writing known as Ogham by which letters were notched so as to form a stroke alphabet on the edges of memorial stones. The distribution of

[1] Hugh Williams, *Christianity in Early Britain* (Oxford, 1912).

[2] At Whithorn in Galloway we have the coming of St. Ninian who dedicated his newly established church there to St. Martin of Tours.

Ogham-inscribed stones shows that the alphabet must have originated in southern Ireland, and people using this script migrated to south-west Wales in large numbers, and some too, to north-west Wales and beyond. The script has been deciphered and thereby has increased enormously the philologist's knowledge of Old Irish. The important issue from the point of view of the present thesis is that in Ireland the Ogham stones have the inscription in Ogham alone, while in Britain, and especially in south-west Wales, there are numerous examples of bilingual stones, that is, stones with inscriptions commemorating the same person in both Ogham and Latin. Dr. Nash-Williams has expressed the opinion that if the individuals recorded on the Ogham stones were not already Christians when they came into Wales, they certainly became Christians soon after their entry. It would appear, therefore, that the Christian *peregrini* arriving from Gaul and the contemporary Irish settlers in west Wales came into close cultural contact with each other. We shall have more to say about this aspect of the question later.

If we direct attention first of all to the Gallic immigrants, we shall not be surprised to find that they brought with them into Wales much of the Roman culture of their home-land. One of their memorials at Penmachno in Caernarvonshire states that it was set up ' in the time of Justinus the Consul.'[1]   Justinus was consul in 540 A.D. and the use of his name was limited on the continent to monuments in the Lyon district. He was the last consul whose name appears on inscriptions in the western world. This reference to Justinus not only dates the inscription and indicates its associations with the Lyon area but also shows that this thoroughly Roman culture was carried into Wales. Indeed, a nearby inscription mentions a *magistratus* and a *civis* indicating an ordered system of government on the Roman model in north-west Wales in sub-Roman times.[2]   In

---

[1] V. E. Nash-Williams, op. cit., No. 104.
[2] V. E. Nash-Williams, op. cit., No. 103.

this Gallic-derived Christian-Roman atmosphere in both north-west and south-west Wales it is easy to understand how strong would be the appeal of the many legends that had gathered around the name of the former Roman Emperor Magnus Maximus (and his Welsh wife, Helena), who had set out from Wales to don the Imperial purple, and who had afterwards befriended that great figure of Gallic monasticism St. Martin of Tours. Here we have a good example of the way in which cultures entering Wales from without soon amalgamate with those of the native folk. The details of the story of the Emperor Maximus and the Empress Helena are worthy of further examination as they would appear to have had much to do with the beginnings of Celtic Christianity in Wales.

It is thought that Magnus Maximus (or Maxen Wledig as he became known in later Welsh tradition) held some high position in the Roman government of Western Britain before he was proclaimed Emperor in 383. Helena, (Elen Luyddog), his wife, was reputed to have had associations with Segontium, the Roman station near Caernarfon. It was Magnus Maximus who had denuded Wales of its Roman garrison in 383, and having passed over from Britain to the continent held his Imperial Court at Trèves. While there, he and his wife were in close touch with St. Martin of Tours.[1] Legend has it that after the defeat and death of her husband in 388 Helena returned to Wales and was regarded there as a saint. In the light of the archaeological background sketched in this chapter there is nothing improbable in this story.[2] Whatever the true facts may have been, Magnus Maximus and his wife Helena captured the imagination of the Welsh storytellers for centuries to come. As St. Elen, Helena has several churches dedicated to her in Wales. Among others we find Llanelen in Monmouthshire ; Llanelen near Llanrhidian in west Gower ; Bletherston church in Pembrokeshire is dedicated to her, and there was formerly a Capel

[1] Sulpicius Severus, *Dialogues* ii. 6 and *Vita S. Martini.*
[2] See an important footnote by V. E. Nash-Williams, op. cit., p. 7, Note 1.

C

Elen in the parish of Penrhosllugwy in Anglesey. She became not only a saint herself but also the mother of saints. Constantine (Cystennin ap Maxen Wledig) was the most important of her sons and he, naturally got confused with Constantine the Great, whose mother bore the same name. There is a Llangystennin (now known as Welsh Bicknor) in Herefordshire[1] and another Llangystennin in Caernarvonshire, twenty miles east of Llanbeblig, which bears the name of another son of Helena—Peblig (Lat. Publicus). Fig. 2 shows the distribution of the dedications to reputed members of the family of Maxen Wledig based on data given in the first volume of Baring Gould and Fisher's *Lives of the British Saints* together with holy wells and other sites traditionally associated with saints of this lineage.[2] While all these saints may be neither blood relations nor contemporaries, and although they may even not be historical characters, the map indicates the areas where traditions regarding these semi-legendary families have survived in a religious context. It is worthy of note that dedications to members of the family of Maxen Wledig are for the most part in areas where Gallo-Roman memorials are found (see Figs. 1 and 2). Particularly noticeable are the western concentrations on both maps, as well as extensions of the distribution pattern eastward from south-western into south-eastern Wales and from north-west Wales into the Conway valley. It is significant, however, that in south-eastern Wales there is evidence of the Maxen Wledig cult in Monmouthshire and western Herefordshire where there are few early Christian inscribed stones belonging to group I, and little evidence of the Maxen cult in Brycheiniog where there are many inscribed stones of the early period. Reference will be made to these matters later. Enough has been said to indicate that the distribution patterns formed by both the group I Early Christian inscribed stones and the cult of the Maxen family in south

---

[1] A. W. Wade-Evans, *Welsh Christian Origins*, 1934, p. 57.

[2] S. Baring Gould and J. Fisher, *Lives of the British Saints*, 1907, Vol. I, Table II, p. 90.

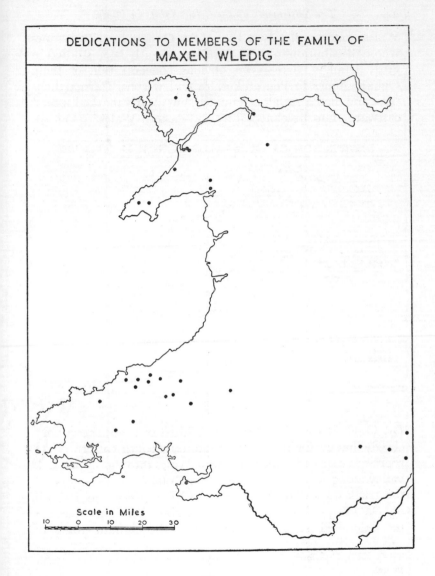

DEDICATIONS TO MEMBERS OF THE FAMILY OF
MAXEN WLEDIG

Scale in Miles

Fig. 2

Wales conforms closely to that of the Ogham inscribed stones whose distribution in these parts has recently been studied in great detail.   There is an obvious concentration of these Ogham stones in Pembrokeshire and western Carmarthenshire and then a rather attenuated, but clearly marked spread eastwards into Brecknockshire and eastern Wales.   (Fig. 3).

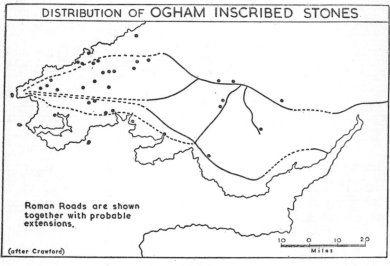

Fig. 3

Dr. O. G. S. Crawford's map published in 1936[1] shows very clearly that the Ogham inscribed stones of south-eastern Wales represent a spread from south-west Wales into the upper Usk valley along what remained of the Roman road system and the track-ways that are thought to have connected it with St. David's peninsula.[2]   Later Dr. Nash-Williams made a more detailed study and showed how the Ogham stones of

[1] O. G. S. Crawford, ' Western Seaways ' in *Custom is King* (Oxford, 1936), p. 190.
[2] The Roman road system in Wales may be said to be contained within the quadrilateral formed by Caerlleon, Maridunum, Segontium and Deva.   Dr. Crawford has added for the peninsula area of West Wales a series of suggested trackways (based on Ogilby's routes in the 17th century) linking the Roman road system with St. David's headland in the extreme western parts of Pembrokeshire (see Figs. 3 and 4).

Brecknockshire were linked with those of south-west Wales
by way of the Roman road leading from Llandovery in
Carmarthenshire to Y Gaer near Brecon.[1] The surviving
topographical evidence of the cult of the saints traditionally
claiming descent from St. Helena and Maximus in south
Wales suggests that similar routes provide the links between
the dedications to these saints in Herefordshire and Monmouthshire and in south-west Wales respectively.

The Roman road system in south Wales together with
the trackways that are thought to have connected it with
western Pembrokeshire may lie behind other early dedication-distribution patterns.[2] Crawford notes a point
which is well worth pursuing. With the aid of interpretive
notes by Egerton Phillimore he draws attention to the
description in the *De Situ Brecheniauc* (a 12th century manuscript preserving much older traditions) of the way Marchell
daughter of Tewdrig and mother of Brychan Brycheiniog
(who gave his name to the present county of Brecknockshire) journeyed in the early 5th century to Ireland to marry
Amlech. Her party is said to have travelled from Llan-
faes in Brecknockshire through Glansefin (Llansefin) (which
is at or near Llangadog in the Tywi valley) by way of
Meidrim in western Carmarthenshire to embark at Porth
Mawr, the harbour for St. David's, in western Pembrokeshire. Here we have indicated precisely the same route
(but followed in the opposite direction) as that already
envisaged for the inscribed stones, Ogham writing, and the
cult of the Saints. We know also that this early post-
Roman kingdom of Brycheiniog had very strong Irish
associations. The above story and the presence of the
Ogham stones is sufficient to indicate this, so that the
present view would be that Tewdrig (the founder of the

[1] Presidential Address to the Cardiff Naturalist Society, 1947.

[2] There is now available abundant evidence for the fact that Roman roads,
continued to be used in Wales for long periods (possibly until the early part of
the 7th century) after the withdrawal of the Roman troops. (See Aileen
Fox, *Camb. Arch. Assoc. Centenary Volume*, 1946, 'Early Christian Period', p. 109
and again by the same author *Arch. Camb*, 1939, p. 40. For a statement on the
English evidence see J. N. L. Myres, *Antiquity*, IX, 1935, p. 456.

kingdom) must have been a leader of one of the numerous bands of Irish adventurers who entered south-west Wales after the withdrawal of the Roman garrisons from the West, and who had pushed on to the eastward to establish his kingdom in the upper Usk basin. As the foregoing evidence tends to suggest, it was not long before the newly arrived Christianity from Gaul spread in from the West in much the same way as these Irish settlers had done, or, possibly, were still continuing to do at this time. In any case, Marchell's son Brychan of Brycheiniog appears in the hagiological literature of the Middle Ages as the progenitor of a prodigiously large family of Saints—both sons and daughters. As is to be expected, no two lists of his reputed children or grandchildren that have come down to us agree either regarding their names or their total number, but if we take, for the sake of argument, the list of his reputed sons alone, as recorded in the most ancient manuscript we possess[1] and then plot the churches and chapels dedicated to them, we get an interesting dedication-distribution (Fig. 4). Not all his saintly sons have churches now

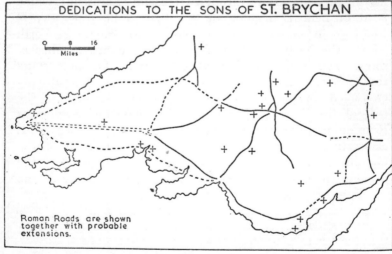

DEDICATIONS TO THE SONS OF ST. BRYCHAN

Roman Roads are shown together with probable extensions.

Fig. 4

[1] Vesp. A. XIV.

dedicated to them—five alone fall into this category namely Arthen, Berwyn, Clydwyn, Cynog and Dingad. A similar distribution pattern would be obtained if dedications to the saintly daughters of Brychan were mapped. The relationship of these dedications to the Roman road system and the routes leading therefrom to the western seas, as suggested by Crawford, is remarkably clear. We have, thus, every reason to associate the establishment of these and other churches dedicated to the children of Brychan with an early re-diffusion of Celtic Christianity from Brycheiniog in the fifth and sixth centuries.[1]

The picture just described would appear to be still further clarified by the evidence derived from an early Christian inscribed stone at Eglwys Gymyn in south-western Carmarthenshire. The site on which this stone was found lies near to the southernmost of the westward running routes shown on Fig. 4, just after it has crossed the Taf. The stone is inscribed in Roman capitals AVITORIA FILIA CUNIGNI [Avitoria daughter of Cunignus (lies here)] and again in Ogham *Inigena Cunigni Avittoriges* [(The Stone) of the daughter of Cunignos, Avittoriga].[2] Cynin was either a son or a grandson of Brychan Brycheiniog and it would appear that he must have helped to evangelise this territory in south-western Carmarthenshire, for his name appears a second time on an inscribed stone at Newchurch not far away,[3] while the church at Llangynin in the same locality is dedicated to him. At Eglwys Gymyn, therefore, we have a memorial stone inscribed with the name of an historical or quasi-historical personage. This in itself is an all-too-rare occurrence. Further, the name of the individual occurs in the lists of Brychan's descendants and appropriately enough the memorial was found near to one of the important westward running routes and inscribed in both scripts as befitted this half-Irish family.

[1] C.f. the argument as presented by Sir John Lloyd in the *History of Carmarthenshire* (Cardiff, 1935), Vol. I, p. 118.
[2] V. E. Nash-Williams, op. cit. No. 142.
[3] V. E. Nash-Williams, op. cit. No. 172.

Another facet of the Brychan tradition tends to confirm the arguments already put forward for the beginnings of Christianity in Wales. It concerns a saint known, significantly, in Wales as Brynach Wyddel (Brynach the Irishman). A 'Life' of this saint appears among several others in the British Museum manuscript Vesp. A. XIV. There we are told that Brynach was a *periglor* (lit. 'a soulfriend') or chaplain of Brychan's and seems to have married one of his many saintly daughters.[1] We are not concerned in this work with the accuracy of these details but only with the fact that there is a traditional association between Brynach and Brychan. The distribution of the Brynach cult in Wales is shown on Fig. 5. It supports the state-

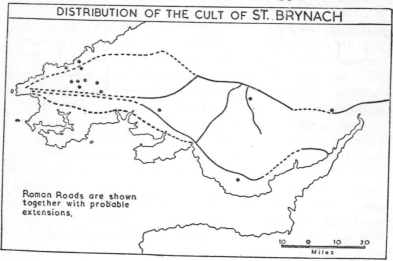

DISTRIBUTION OF THE CULT OF ST. BRYNACH

Roman Roads are shown together with probable extensions.

Miles

Fig. 5

ment that he was Brynach *Wyddel*, while the overall distribution is similar to that of the Ogham inscribed stones (Fig. 3). Both are related to the ancient trackways and Roman roads leading from the Western Seas. Unfortunately, Brynach's name is not recorded anywhere in Ogham characters but we have the very interesting fact that in his

[1] Baring Gould and Fisher, *Lives of the British Saints*, Vol. I, p. 321.

most important church at Nevern (Nyfer) in north Pembrokeshire there are three Ogham inscribed stones. While
by no means all Ogham inscribed stones are found in or
near to the precincts of Celtic churches in Wales (and those
that are may have been removed there by archaeologists
in relatively recent times for safety), yet we should not overlook the fact that there are several instances in Ireland of
Ogham stones being set up near the oratory or monastic
establishment of a Celtic saint. This was the case at St.
Manchan's cell near Dingle in Co. Kerry.[1] If the Nevern
stones have really been associated with the precints of the
church throughout the centuries the parallel with the Irish
examples supports the argument.

Before leaving the cult of Brychan and his children it
remains to consider another Welsh saint—Peulin, Paulinus
(St. Paul de Leon) whose cult is closely linked with that of
the children of Brychan in Wales and Brittany. Peulin
is traditionally associated with north Carmarthenshire and
an inscribed stone found near Cynwyl Caeo bears his name.
It is inscribed in Roman capitals with two barbarous
hexameters extolling the saint in eulogistic terms. This
type of memorial can be paralleled in classical and contemporary Gaulish and continental inscriptions of the 5th
and 6th century, and Dr. Nash-Williams dates this inscription about 550 A.D. In addition we possess a really
ancient ' Life ' of Paulinus. His cult was carried over to
Brittany and as St. Paul de Leon his story was written
down by a monk called Wrmonoc in 884 A.D. This 'Life '
has been carefully analysed by the late Canon Doble.[2]
Nevertheless, the most important point for our thesis is a
topographical one, namely that in the parish of Llanddingad in northern Carmarthenshire, in the zone of
contact between the south-west peninsula of Wales and the
Roman road system, there are two chapels dedicated to
St. Peulin, one at Capel Peulin and the other at Nant-y-

---

[1] R. A. S. Macalister, *Corpus Inscriptionum Insularum Celticarum*, No. 170.
[2] G. H. Doble, *St. Paul of Leon*, Cornish Saints' Series, No. 46 (Lampeter,
1941). See also R. D. Williams, *Y Llan*, Gorff. 18, 1952.

Bai, and also a holy well called Ffynnon Beulin.   This is a most significant area in which to find evidences of such an early and well-authenticated Celtic saint for it is noteworthy that the parish of Llanddingad in addition to its situation, contains the site of a former Roman station, and its church is dedicated to St. Dingad, one of the traditional children of Brychan Brycheiniog.   Seven and a half miles away from these Peulin dedications in Llanddingad and in a position corresponding very well with the description in the ' Life,' is Llanddeusant (the ' Llan ' of the Two Saints) said to be those of his two brothers Notolius and Potolius.   Then the only other church in Wales dedicated to St. Peulin is that of Llangors in Brecknockshire.   It contains two chapels, one called Llanbeulin and the other Llan y Deuddeg Sant (The ' Llan ' of the Twelve Saints). There is a reference to the Twelve Saints in Wrmonoc's ' Life.'   It seems, therefore, that Peulin, like the saintly Children of Brychan and possibly of Maxen Wledig too, used the Roman road connecting Llandovery to Y Gaer at Brecon and beyond.   As Doble puts it ' the coincidences between Wrmonoc's statements and the information from Welsh topography are most striking and can not be fortuitous.'[1]

We are now in a position to summarize the argument set out in the preceding pages.   The archaeological evidence shows that Gallo-Roman Christian emigrées must have arrived by sea in considerable numbers on both the south-western and the north-western peninsulas of Wales and then spread inland using ancient routeways which led them on to what remained of the net-work of Roman military roads. The traditions of Gallic monasticism which appear to have gathered around the reputed descendants of Magnus Maximus flourished in this neo-Roman setting and helped to lay the foundations of Christian Wales.   In time it would appear that South Wales forged ahead of the North, in spite of the fact that Celtic Christianity might have taken

---

[1] G. H. Doble, op. cit., p. 30.

root very early in the Segontium area. The difference between North and South Wales is also clearly marked in the relatively small number of Irish proto-Christian immigrants using the seaways, the ancient trackways and the Roman roads in the North as compared with the South. There are also fewer Ogham inscribed stones in North Wales than in South Wales. Furthermore, there does not appear to be any parallel in the North for the whole complex centred around the family of Brychan Brycheiniog and their associates (such as Brynach and Peulin) in the South. It is interesting to speculate at this juncture whether the different activity witnessed in the North and South respectively may not be due to the disturbances caused in the North by the coming of the Sons of Cunedda. Although we are not certain whether the Cunedda people were Christians when they arrived in North Wales, we do know that great saintly families were soon to arise in this part of Wales and to claim descent from their Princes. These were the saints who were largely responsible for building up the Celtic Church in North Wales and whose influence later penetrated southward. Whichever way we look at the Cunedda invasion nothing stands out more clearly than the sharp distinction made in Welsh hagiology between the Brychan and the Cunedda families, thus emphasizing the deep-rooted cultural differences between North and South Wales even at this remote time.

We may now return to the story of St. Tathan at Caerwent with which we began this narrative. In light of the contrast between North and South Wales which has just been emphasized it may be worth while reflecting on a suggestion made by Wade-Evans[1] that Tathan may well have been one of the Irish of what is now Caernarvonshire, perhaps Tathal of Caer Dathal in Arfon, in which case he would have been from among the Irish settlers amidst the Gallo-Roman Christians of the North before the coming of the Sons of Cunedda. As an Irishman he might even be fleeing from their conquests and, moving thence by sea,

[1] A. W. Wade-Evans, op. cit., p. 119.

set himself up anew in Caer-went. This would mean that south-east Wales was receiving by sea chance contacts with the same Goidelic-Gallo-Roman Christianity that was spreading into the area simultaneously by the overland routes from Brycheiniog. Reflecting on the evidence as set out in this chapter it would appear to be fairly certain that the land routes across south Wales from the west were in greater use in this immediate post-Roman period than the sea-route along the southern coast, thus making the traditional voyage of St. Tathan somewhat exceptional.

We cannot conclude a chapter on Celtic Christianity which is entitled *In the Beginning* without some reference to St. Germanus of Auxerre. Most authorities on the period ascribe the beginnings of Celtic Christianity in Western Britain to this great saint who had made famous missions to these islands against Pelagianism in the fifth century.[1] No one, however, knows his precise destinations in Britain or even where he landed. Crawford[2] has suggested that he may have taken a western route and that he had objectives in the west as well as in the east. While there is much to be said in favour of this suggestion, it must be remembered that the many churches in Wales that claim to be dedicated to St. Germanus of Auxerre under the Welsh name of Garmon can not justify their claims on modern philological evidence. Sir Ifor Williams[3] has shown that the Welsh Garmon can not be derived regularly from Germanus and we are, therefore, forced to conclude that the group of church dedications in Powys to St. Garmon are to another saint and not to St. Germanus of Auxerre That Garmon was a saint who laboured in Powys is brought out clearly by the close correspondence between the distribution of his cult and that of other Powysian saints (see page 79). Here, then, we have a good example of the dangers involved in an uncritical application of the dedication-distribution method.

[1] See, for example, R. G. Collingwood and J. N. L. Myres' *Roman Britain and the English Settlements* (1936), p. 312, and G. H. Doble, *St. Paul of Leon* (1941), p. 3.
[2] O. G. S. Crawford, op. cit., p. 187.
[3] Ifor Williams, ' Hen Chwedlau', *Trans. Hon. Soc. Cymmrod*, 1946-47.

CHAPTER II

THE SOUTH-EASTERN CULTS

IF we adopt the conventional division of Britain into a Highland and a Lowland Zone separated by a line joining the mouth of the Tees to that of the Exe, we appreciate at a glance that the position of south-east Wales is that of a western projection of Lowland Britain into the Highland Zone. This all-important fact of physical geography is clearly reflected in the unmistakable association of this region throughout the ages with the cultural life of Lowland Britain.

Prior to the Roman conquest there had been a marked infiltration of Belgic culture from south-eastern Britain into these parts. Dobunic coins are found in the Plain of Gwent and along the Hereford—Brecknockshire lowlands. This coinage was struck by the Dobuni—a Cotswold non-Belgic tribe which had adopted an inscribed coinage in imitation of that of the Commian Belgae of Wessex[1] (Fig. 6.) After the Roman conquest of south-eastern England in the second quarter of the first century A.D. Belgic influences became more marked in these areas. Belgic pottery has been found in hill-forts at Llanmelin, Lydney and Sudbrook in Monmouthshire.[2] This infiltration of Belgic culture may even have culminated in the arrival of occasional drafts of Belgic refugees in south-east Wales at the time of Caratacus's withdrawal to the West. The Roman conquest left a marked impression on the area. In the more peaceful times of the second century, the Roman town of Caerwent (Venta Silurum) was located here, and in the countryside around were established several Roman villas—residences on the estates of prosperous Roman or Romano-

---

[1] See *Antiquity* VII, 1933, pp. 281-2. Map VIII.
[2] V. E. Nash-Williams, *Arch. Camb.* 1933, p. 237 and 1939, p. 42, also R. E. M. Wheeler's report on a site in Lydney Park, Gloucestershire, *Arch. Camb.* 1921.

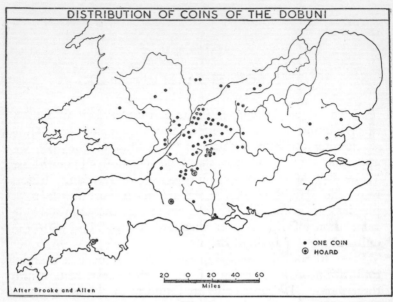

DISTRIBUTION OF COINS OF THE DOBUNI

● ONE COIN
◉ HOARD

20 0 20 40 60
Miles

After Brooke and Allen

Fig. 6

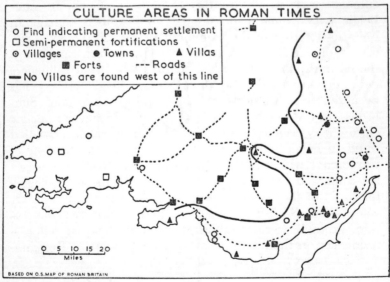

CULTURE AREAS IN ROMAN TIMES

○ Find indicating permanent settlement
□ Semi-permanent fortifications
◉ Villages   ● Towns   ▲ Villas
▣ Forts   --- Roads
━ No Villas are found west of this line

0 5 10 15 20
Miles

BASED ON O.S. MAP OF ROMAN BRITAIN

Fig. 7

British landlords. Their distribution in South Wales demarcates the south-eastern cultural sub-province shown on Fig. 7. This sub-province is, in fact, but a western extension of the Roman zone of civil occupation which was roughly coincident with the Lowlands of south-eastern Britain. Its frontiers in south-eastern Wales are sharply defined by the hill-country to the north and west, which can be shown on archaeological evidence to have experienced little of the fullness of Roman life character-istic of the Lowlands. In the hill-country the occupation was essentially military in character ; the countryside being intersected by a network of military roads linking up the scattered forts. Finally, beyond the western margins of the military road system in Wales lay extensive territor-ies that experienced less contact with Roman life and institutions than either of the regions previously described. When in due course the Roman hold on Britain weakened, south-eastern Wales would appear to have received at the beginning of the fifth century refugees comparable to the Belgae of early Roman times, escaping now from the resulting chaos in south-eastern Britain. It has already been suggested that among such refugees were the builders of the very late Romano-British church at Caer-went on the sea-plain. We must not, however, overlook the advantages offered by the deeply broken country further north, between the Wye and the Severn to such refugees (including possibly some Christian colonies) migrating from the Silchester-Cirencester area. It is clear from Fig. 6 that the coinage of the Cotswold-based Dobuni five centuries earlier had certainly reached both areas.

This chapter is concerned with the growth of Celtic Christianity in these parts. We noted previously that cultural influences emanating from the westward could reach this area either directly by sea, or by using the over-land routes across South Wales, and that there were strong reasons for thinking that the overland routes were the ones used by the Gallo-Roman Christians as well as the Irish settlers in eastern Wales. The Roman road leading from

Maridunum in the west up the Tywi valley to the modern
Llandovery continued thence into the Vale of Usk, passed
the Brecon Gaer to contact this south-eastern Borderland
by way of Abergavenny and Monmouth. This route was
balanced, as it were, to the southward by a coastal road,
which, after passing inland from Maridunum to Loughor,
hereafter traversed the 'Vale' of Glamorgan towards
Caerlleon and Caer-went, and ultimately crossed the
Severn estuary to Aust on the Somerset side (see Fig. 7).
The map showing the Early Christian monuments of Gallo-
Roman age (Fig. 1) shows the northern route to have
been more important in bringing this culture to south-
eastern Wales than the southern route. It led ultimately
into the middle Wye valley where, beyond the river, some
two miles E.S.E. of Ross lay the ancient city of Ariconium,
which in the fifth century gave its name to the small Celtic
kingdom of Erging which was roughly co-terminous with
the hundred of Archenfield in Hereford. Near to Ariconium, and situated in a conspicuous meander of the Wye,
lies Welsh Bicknor, formerly Llangystennin, thus preserving
traces of the cult of Constantine—(son of Elen and Maxen
Wledig), which, if our argument is correct, had also penetrated into these parts from the westward along the former
Roman roads. It seems very likely, therefore, that it was
in these parts that the vanguard of the western-sea derived
Gallo-Roman Christianity, with its strong eremetical
tendencies and possibly its 'Maxen Wledig' traditions
was, in the early fifth century, in close contact with
refugees from Christian communities in Roman Britain.
It is in Archenfield, too, that we find a cluster of dedications
to St. Dubricius (Dyfrig) (see Fig. 8A). His chief church
was at Hentland (4 miles W.N.W. of Ross). The present
village is located on an original Roman site. We have
a very early reference to Dyfrig in the *Vita Samsonis* which
was written by a monk of the monastery of Dol in Brittany
possibly at the beginning of the seventh century.[1] In

[1] G. H. Doble, *St. Dubricius*, Welsh Saints' Series, No. 2, 1943, p. 1.

chapter 13 of this work we are told of the *papa* Dubricius coming to Illtud's famous monastery on a Sunday to ordain Samson deacon, two other brethren being ordained presbyters at the same time. Four manuscripts of this early 'Life' refer to Dyfrig as *Dubricio papa*, and another four as either *Dubritio* or *Dubricio episcopo*. The influence of Romano-British Christianity seems clearly indicated. All this is five hundred years before the re-modelling of traditions concerning him and the fabrication of others in the *Liber Landavensis*. Later traditions make him a pupil of St. Germanus of Auxerre, which may indicate that he had always been considered as an early saint, but equally significant is the tradition that he was a descendant of King Erb and in that way linked mythologically with the family of Maxen Wledig.

Two dedications to Dyfrig lie beyond the major concentration in Archenfield. He is patron of Gwenddwr, south of Builth in Brecknockshire. This church lies in the immediate vicinity of a Roman road thereby suggesting, as in the case of the Sons of Brychan, that the former Roman roads were widely used in the re-diffusion of Celtic Christianity from this part of the Welsh Borderland. The other outlying dedication to him is that of the parish church of Porlock on the north coast of Somerset. It is called *ecclesia S. Dubricii* in the foundation deed of the Harrington chantry in 1476 and shows that either St. Dubricius himself, or monks of one of his houses, played some part in initiating the great missionary expansion of later times. This expansion starting in south-eastern Wales, reached the Severn Sea and moving then down the opposite shores of the Channel covered not only the coast of Somerset, but, later, the whole of the south-west peninsula and even Brittany with churches and monasteries, many of which still bear the names of their Welsh founders. There is, therefore, a great deal in the surviving topographical evidence to suggest that the immediate origins of Celtic Christianity in southern Britain lay near the present south-

D

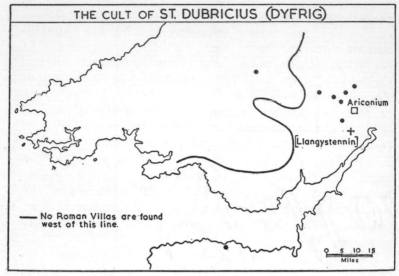

Fig. 8A

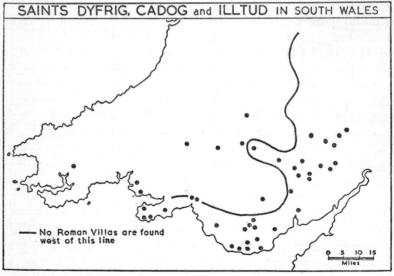

Fig 8B.

eastern borders of Wales, in a region where, in the Dark Ages, the re-introduced Gallo-Roman Christianity from the West came into contact with Christian refugees from south-eastern Britain. Such was the cultural environment in which St. Dubricius laboured and here churches dedicated to him are chiefly found. We agree with Doble who on essentially different evidence concludes that Dyfrig was undoubtedly ' one of the earliest of the Welsh saints.'[1]

The distribution of dedications to other well-known south-eastern saints such as Saints Cadog and Illtud follows much the same general pattern as that to St. Dyfrig. Certain features, however, of these distributions suggest that we are dealing with saints of a slightly later period. (Fig. 8B).

St. Cadog is obviously one of the builders of Christian Wales and, in addition, his cult has spread far and wide throughout the Celtic lands. His father is said to be Gwynllyw—a princeling of Gwent—and his mother to be in the lineage of Brychan Brycheiniog. There is an air of authenticity about his ancestry which stands out in sharp contrast with the obviously spurious ancestry of many of the later saints. His dedications in south-east Wales tend to gather in two clusters—one around Llangattock-nigh-Usk in the ancient territory of Gwent, and the other in the eastern part of the Vale of Glamorgan in the ancient territory of Glywysig. This latter cluster focuses upon Cadog's most famous centre at Llancarfan (Nant Carban). When we pass from these major clusters and consider the saint's outlying dedications in South Wales we note that their association with a Roman context becomes specially marked. Cadog's churches at Gelli-gaer and Caerlleon are outstanding examples. In addition, we see that he (or one of his immediate disciples) made use of both the inland (northern) and the coastal (southern) Roman roads leading to the westward. His cult, possibly because it was stronger, or because it came later, or persisted longer, reached further to the westward along the inland route than did that of Dyfrig. We find Cadog dedications and place-

[1] G. H. Doble, op. cit., p. 6.

names strung outward along the general line of this route from Llangadog Crucywel via Llansbyddyd (near Brecon) towards Llangadog below Llandovery in the Tywi valley.[1] In contrast to St. Dyfrig, St. Cadog or his followers seem to have used the southern or coastal route to the west as well. This would appear to be a natural corollary following upon the location of Llancarfan in the Vale of Glamorgan. There are, or were, chapels dedicated to St. Cadog at Cadoxton near Neath where an important N.E.—S.W. link-road joins the main coastal road ; at Cheriton and Portheinon, on either side of the Gower peninsula, and another just to the north of Kidwelly. This latter site is not associated in any way with the Roman road, but lies almost alongside of the ancient trackway referred to in the previous chapter, that leaves the Roman road near Loughor and runs due westward making for the fords across the Gwendraeth-Tywi-Taf estuaries (see Fig. 4). Along this trackway further westward, in Pembrokeshire, is St. Cadog's chapel at Llawhaden (Llanrhiadain).

These western extensions of the Cadogian dedications are suggestive of the fact that either the saint himself or some of his followers were in direct contact with the main western-sea routes. That such was the case is abundantly clear from the traces that still remain of the cult of St. Cadog from western Scotland to the Morbihan. There was a Llan-gadog in the parish of Amlwch in the north-eastern corner of Anglesey, while far away to the northwards the church of Cambuslang on the Clyde above Glasgow is dedicated to him.[2] In the opposite direction there are evidences of the saint's influence in Cornwall in the ruins of a very important chapel dedicated to him in the parish of Pad-stow near the shores of Harlyn Bay, while across the sea in Brittany he had a widespread popular cult emanating, it would appear, from his celebrated monastery on the Ilê

---

[1] The church at Llangadog is dedicated to St. David (see p.63).

[2] W. J. Watson, ' The Cult of St. Cadoc in Scotland', *Scottish Gaelic Studies* (1927), Vol. II, pp. 1-12.

de Cado in the Sea of Etel, just north of the Quiberon peninsula.[1]

The general distribution of the cult of St. Illtud bears a close similarity to that of St. Cadog. After St. Cadog, St. Illtud is the most important saint whose cult is based on the south-eastern province. Like St. Cadog he is also referred to in the *Vita Samsonis* and is said there to be a pupil of St. Germanus of Auxerre. Traditions concerning him are found also in later ' Lives ' and he possesses a *Vita* of his own in the British Museum Ms. Vespasian A. xiv.[2] The centre of his cult was at Llanilltud Fawr (Eng. Llantwit Major) in the south-western part of the Vale of Glamorgan. The site is in close proximity to a Roman villa (see page 124), but there is no very obvious association between the siting of other churches dedicated to St. Illtud in south Glamorgan and the material remains of Roman civilization. The important point is the general correspondence that exists between the area with Illtud-Cadog churches and that which shows strongly developed civil life in South Wales in Roman times. Illtud has really only one cluster of dedications in south-east Wales rather than two as was the case with St. Cadog (see Fig. 9 A and B). Nevertheless, the inland (northern) and the coastal (southern) routes to the west were apparently utilized much in the same way as by St. Cadog. Dedications to St. Illtud occur at Llanhamlach, four miles east of Brecon and at Llanilltud (sometimes called Capel Illtud) in the ancient parish of Defynnog. The chapel is on the mountain side directly above the Roman road leading from Neath to Brecon. There is no direct topographical evidence of the Illtud cult further to the westward, but it is most significant that at Llanhamlach Illtud would appear to be in very close contact with such western based cults as that of St. Peulin, for the church of the neighbouring parish of Llangors is dedicated to St. Paulinus. Incidents in the *Vita Pauli*

---

[1] G. H. Doble, *St. Cadoc in Cornwall and Brittany*, Cornish Saints' Series, No. 40 (Truro, 1937).

[2] G. H. Doble, *St. Iltut* (University of Wales Press : Cardiff, 1944).

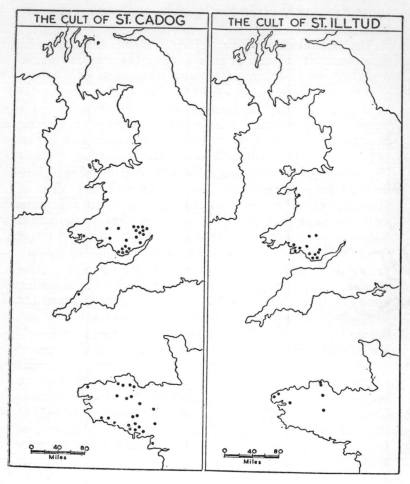

Fig. 9A   Fig. 9B

connect Illtud with Peulin while the topographical evidence
both in Wales and in Brittany would appear to substantiate
these traditions.

On the southern route across South Wales Illtud is
culted just across the river from Cadog at Llantwit-juxta-
Neath (Llanilltud Nedd). In Gower he is patron of
Ilston (Llanilltud Gŵyr) and Oxwich on the southern
face of the peninsula, while there is a holy well bearing his
name on the north coast in the parish of Llanrhidian.
Leaving the Roman road (but continuing westward along
the same track as that presumably followed by the propa-
gators of the cult of St. Cadog) we reach the church of
Pen-bre which is dedicated to St. Illtud. Some workers
have seen fainter traces of his cult further westward in
Pembrokeshire,[1] but there can be no doubt at all about
its presence at Llanelltud on the banks of the western flowing Mawddach near to Dolgellau in Merionethshire. It is
only by assuming the use of the western sea-routes that we
can account for a dedication to St. Illtud so located (see
p. 47). Unlike St. Cadog, St. Illtud does not seem to have
any dedications in Cornwall but he had a widespread cult
in the dioceses of Léon, Tréguier and Vannes in Brittany
(Fig. 9B).

Before we attempt to review the south-eastern cults as a
whole there is a matter regarding Illtud's most northerly
dedication at Llanelltud which has not hitherto been fully
appreciated. Professor Henry Lewis has recently pointed
out[2] that the Welsh or Brittonic form of Illtud's name is
undoubtedly Elltud and the corresponding Irish form would
be Iltuath. He then goes on to state that the late Sir
John Rhŷs made the interesting observation that the use
of the Irish form in south-east Wales is attested by the
name of Lan-yltwyt or -iltwyt which was the name of St.
Illtud's famous monastery before it was reduced to Llantwit. The presence of the Goidelic form of the name
throughout South Wales and the occurrence of the

[1] G. H. Doble, ibid, pp. 11, 38, 39, etc.
[2] G. H. Doble, ibid, p. 33 (Note).

Brittonic form in the North may indicate not only the intense Brittonic character of the Cunedda conquest, but, more significantly, the fact that early Celtic Christianity in south-east Wales functioned in a strong Goidelic atmosphere—as presumably was the case in primitive Brycheiniog. There is nothing in the evidence, be it archaeological, hagiological, philological or topographical, to contradict the view that these south-eastern cults were derived by the overspill of the very early Celtic Christianity of the Archenfield area and of Brycheiniog into the more Romanized south-eastern lowlands.

We can now review the south-eastern cults as a whole. First and foremost we cannot overlook their essentially ' Roman ' or ' Romano-British ' character, to which reference has already been made. The later medieval traditions concerning the local leaders indicate the persistence of this ' Roman ' orientation to a degree not found among the later Celtic saints in other parts of Wales. We have noted that references to Dubricius indicate a leader more in the tradition of a Roman territorial bishop than a recluse of the Celtic type. Likewise, the writer of the early twelfth century ' Life ' of St. Cadog thinks of him, too, in a strong Roman setting. He is made out to be a direct descendant of a long line of Roman emperors in unbroken succession from Augustus, and to love the work of Virgil and even to regret that he (as a Christian) will be unable to meet the distinguished pagan poet in the Hereafter.

We may, however, be on safer ground in developing this theme if we return once more to the early seventh century *Vita Samsonis*. There we have, possibly, a still more vivid memory of the *magister Eltut*. Young Samson is being taken by his parents to Illtud's famous school at Llanilltud Fawr and the writer of the ' Life ' in introducing Illtud says ' Now this Eltut was the most learned of all the Britons in his knowledge of the Scriptures, both the Old Testament and the New Testament and in every branch of philosophy, poetry and rhetoric, grammar and arithmetic ; and he was most sagacious and gifted with the power of foretelling future events.'[1]   This passage can be interpreted as indicating that St. Illtud might have combined in himself elements derived from such diverse sources as the Christian tradition, the Roman aristocracy, and the pagan priesthood.   Such cultural fusion is exactly what one would have expected on *a priori* grounds to have been characteristic of this region at this time.

Another matter which the student of historical geography cannot overlook is the location of the famous south Glamorgan monasteries with which this story is connected— Llanilltud (Llantwit Major) and Nant Carban (Llancarfan).   They probably functioned as channel ports.[2] They are not directly on the sea coast but lie hidden away in the lower reaches of small river valleys out of sight of sea pirates.   They are, however, near to the main Roman road traversing the South Wales sea-plain and conveniently well up-Channel to provide an easy crossing.   The northern shores of the Bristol Channel lying still further up the estuary were particularly marshy and thus ill-suited for settlement.[3]   With the growing importance of sea traffic as the Dark Ages progressed, these monasteries were well placed to share in the benefits of the important Irish traffic that passed to and from the continent by way of South Wales.   It is particularly worthy of note that the tradition of high scholarship and learning remained with the schools of Illtud and Cadog throughout their long history.   In this way they stand out in sharp contrast to the more westerly placed Celtic monasteries in Wales, where, in spite of their fame in other respects, no such traditions of great learning are associated with them.[4]

There is evidence from prehistoric times that several

---

[1] Quoted by Doble, ibid, p. 1.

[2] O. G. S. Crawford, ' Western Seaways ' in *Custom is King* (Oxford, 1936), pp. 191-2.

[3] It is significant that there are no dedications to any of the saints mentioned in this chapter in the lowlying marshy coastland district between the present-day towns of Cardiff and Newport.

[4] E. G. Bowen, ' The Settlements of the Celtic Saints in South Wales', *Antiquity* XIX, 1945, p. 186.

early cultures had originated in south-east Wales, and it is significant that there is a remarkable similarity between the combined distribution of dedications to Saints Dyfrig, Cadog and Illtud and the patterns resulting from the mapping of objects relating to some of these early cultures. A very clear resemblance exists, for example, between the distribution pattern formed by the find-sites of a Late Bronze Age (1000-500 B.C.) socketed axe, ornamented with three converging ribs, and the known dedications to the above named saints. Fox[1] has shown that the focus

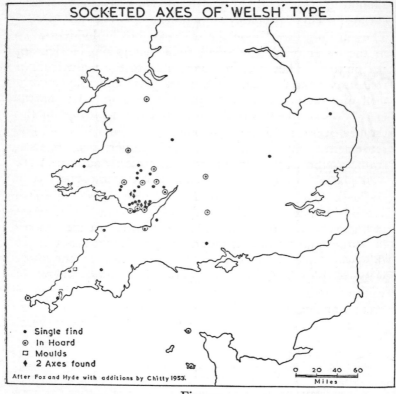

Fig. 10

[1] C. Fox and H. A. Hyde, ' The Llynfawr Hoard', *Antiquaries Journal*, 1939, p. 390.   Plate LXXXI.

of this Late Bronze Age distribution is in south-eastern Wales which is, therefore, claimed to be the centre of origin of this particular school of metallurgy (see Fig. 10). Not only do the focal areas of the prehistoric and Early Christian cultures coincide but the regions affected by the outward spread of both cultures is equally significant. It is clear from Fig. 10 that both the Teifi valley and the upper Dee valley were accessible to south-east Wales by means of the sea-routes at least a thousand years before the Age of the Saints. Against this background the presence of an apparently isolated dedication to St. Illtud in a remote western-facing valley in Merionethshire would appear to be a normal rather than an exceptional occurrence. Likewise, the spread of the South Wales socketed axe into the south-western peninsula of England and across the sea to the Channel Islands is closely paralleled in a later age by the missionary activity of these three Welsh saints (or their followers) in south-west England and in Brittany.

Having sought such early parallels for the distributions of the Dark Ages, it is appropriate also to seek others in later times. In this respect it is worthy of note that much the same area as contained the nucleus of the Dyfrig, Cadog and Illtud dedications emerges in the twelfth century as the diocese of Llandaf. Exactly how the territorial limits of this bishopric came to be defined is a highly complicated story. We know that in the Celtic church there were no diocesan bishops and no dioceses. Nevertheless, with the Norman penetration and the growing power of Canterbury, the country was divided into bishoprics and parishes on the Latin model. At the beginning of the twelfth century, and following in the wake of the Norman Conquest, a Bishop Urban (who owed alleginace to Canterbury) styled himself ' Bishop of Glamorgan.' He presided over the affairs of the church in the country between the river Tawe and the river Wye. It was he who in 1120 began to build a cathedral church at Llandaf Henceforth the bishops of that part of Wales were known.

as Bishops of Llandaf. In exactly the same way as the
Norman bishops of Bangor and St. David's claimed to be
in the line of Saints Deiniol and David respectively so, too,
the bishops of Llandaf claimed to be in the line of St.
Dubricius. The evidence for this claim was supplied by
an elaborate compilation known as the *Liber Landavensis*
written after Urban's death in 1133. It is clearly the
attempt of an ingenious medieval writer to bolster up the
pretensions of the newly constituted See. The writer of
this work, in order to expand still further the claims of the
diocese, brings St. Teilo into the line of Dubrician bishops
supposedly settled at Llandaf in ancient times. On this
authority Llandaf claimed not only all the Dubrician
churches but also the Teilo churches as well, and so when
it came to define its territorial limits, the medieval diocese
of Llandaf found itself in sharp conflict with the claims of
the diocese of Hereford on the one hand, and those of St.
David's on the other.[1] Nevertheless, if we strip the story
of its medieval accretions it is clear that the nucleus of the
territorial bishopric in the later Middle Ages comprised
very much the same area as that in which Saints Dyfrig,
Cadog and Illtud had established the majority of their
churches in earlier times. (Fig. 11). Thus, the persistent
individualism of south-eastern Wales is clearly in evidence
throughout the long period under review in this chapter.

[1] William Rees, *An Historical Atlas of Wales* (Cardiff, 1951). See Plate 33
and p. 30.

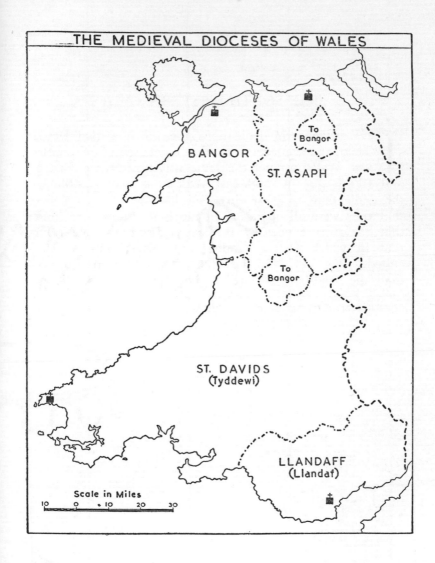

THE MEDIEVAL DIOCESES OF WALES

BANGOR

ST. ASAPH

To Bangor

To Bangor

ST. DAVIDS
(Tyddewi)

LLANDAFF
(Llandaf)

Scale in Miles
10   0   10   20   30

Fig. 11

CHAPTER III

THE SOUTH-WESTERN CULTS

THE evidence of dedications goes to show that Dewi, Teilo and Padarn were the chief saints of south-west Wales in much the same way that Dyfrig, Cadog and Illtud were in south-east Wales. A map combining the dedications to these three south-western saints shows that they were all operating in much the same area, and that the area concerned is clearly distinguishable from that in which Dyfrig, Cadog and Illtud were chiefly culted. (Fig. 12). On the whole, it would be true to say that the traditions regarding both groups are seldom

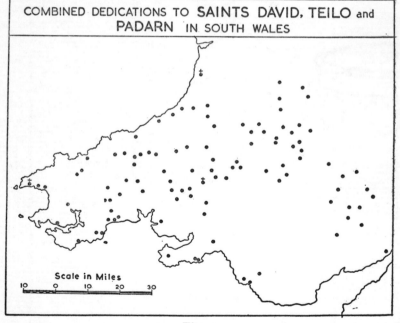

Fig. 12

intermingled in the hagiological literature and that the traditions concerning the three south-western saints imply some sort of co-operation between them. This, at any rate, is the view adopted by leading authorities on the history of Wales.[1] Nevertheless, the material comprising the ' Lives ' of Saints Dewi, Teilo and Padarn is so obviously legendary in character that it cannot be relied upon for a single historical fact, and in many ways the ' Lives ' of these presumably later saints stand out in contrast with the seemingly more genuine biographies of the saints of south-eastern Wales. For instance, the spurious details concerning the parentage of Dewi, as described in his ' Life ' stand out in sharp contrast with the far more reasonable statements made concerning the parentage of Cadog in his ' Life.' Reference, therefore, can be made to such late sources only when they would appear to be recording genuine traditions concerning these saints. Likewise, when we turn to a consideration of the topographical evidence, special care is also necessary in dealing with dedications to Dewi Sant. This is due to his widespread popularity and to the fact that St. David's was regarded as a place of pilgrimage second only to Rome. Later St. David came to be regarded as the patron saint of Wales. This is the kind of atmosphere in which extensive re-culting was likely to occur, and so the present topographical evidence in turn becomes less valuable as a means of indicating the distribution of foundations established during the lifetime of the saint or in the period immediately afterwards. As patron saint it is not surprising that Dewi Sant possesses the largest number of dedications of any Celtic saint in the Principality,[2] yet the distribution of his cult shows one outstanding feature in that there is not a single ancient dedication to him in the whole of North Wales (see Fig. 13). This tends to confirm the view already expressed that when re-culting does take place, as it did in this case, then the

[1] J. E. Lloyd, *A History of Wales*, 3rd Edition (1939), Vol. I, p. 159.
[2] Rice Rees in his *Essay on the Welsh Saints* listed fifty-three dedications in 1836.

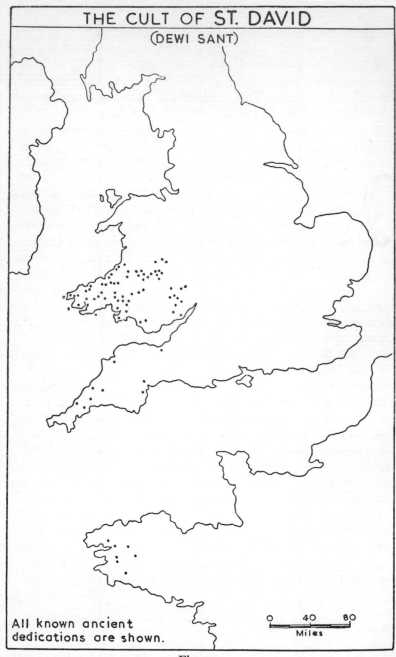

THE CULT OF ST. DAVID
(DEWI SANT)

All known ancient
dedications are shown.

0   40   80
Miles

Fig. 13

tendency is strongest within what must have been the original *patria* of the saint in question.

Before proceeding to discuss the distribution pattern of the dedications to each of these three south-western saints individually, we should note that a map showing dedications to all three together would bring out the importance of the territory formed by what is now Carmarthenshire, Pembrokeshire and Cardiganshire as well as much of modern Brecknockshire, Radnorshire and even Monmouthshire. Taken severally, however, we find that the distribution of dedications to St. Padarn does not follow the same pattern as those of Teilo and Dewi which are mainly responsible for the overall picture.

The Padarn dedications in Wales fall into an eastern and a western group separated by the Central Wales uplands. On the western side we have Llanbadarn Fawr—a mile or so east of Aberystwyth—the metropolis of his cult. Then, in the same county is Llanbadarn Fach (also called Trefeglwys) which lies two miles due east of Llanddewi Aberarth, and Llanbadarn Odwyn about a mile east of Llangeitho. In addition, St. Padarn is the patron of the parish of Pencarreg to the south of the Teifi in northern Carmarthenshire. East of the Central Wales uplands we have three Padarn churches in Radnorshire : Llanbadarn Fawr in the north of the county, Llanbadarn Fynydd in central Radnorshire and Llanbadarn Garreg near the southern borders. (Fig. 14). The name Padarn occurs as an element in place names elsewhere in Wales, but nowhere in a proven hagiological context. It is more likely that the name may have been a fairly common one in Wales as in Brittany. It is significant that the Padarn dedications do not occur in wellmarked clusters as is the case with the south-east Wales saints. They give every indication of being aligned in association with major north to south routeways. It is not difficult to see that the Radnorshire churches are ranged along much the same strip of country as that followed by the Roman road from Y Gaer at Brecon northwards to the

E

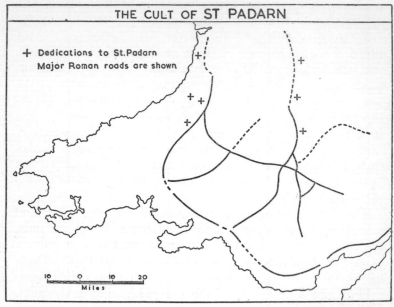

THE CULT OF ST PADARN

+ Dedications to St.Padarn
Major Roman roads are shown

10 0 10 20
Miles

Fig. 14

Roman station at Castell Collen. Similarly, on the western side, the Roman road from Maridunum (Carmarthen), running northwards, passes through the parish of Pencarreg and close to it is the church of which St. Padarn is patron. The road then continues northwards to the Roman station at Llanio. For some miles beyond this spot, and along a section that is traditionally known as Sarn Helen, the remains of the road are very clearly marked. Over the crest of a hill, out of sight of the road, but nevertheless within easy reach of it, stands Llanbadarn Odwyn. Still further north the roadway is not so clearly marked but scholars have been able to trace it swinging north-westward towards the coast and crossing the Ystwyth and Rheidol rivers not far from Llanbadarn Fawr on its way to the next Roman station at Pennal in Merionethshire.[1] Llanbadarn Trefeglwys alone

---

[1] See map of Roman Wales by C. L. Mathew and V. E. Nash-Williams in *The Roman Legionary Fortress at Caerleon, Monmouthshire* (National Museum of Wales : Cardiff, 1939).

appears to lie outside the general orientation of the Roman road system but, even so, we must not overlook the fact that it is situated, like Llanbadarn Fawr itself within easy access of the sea. As has been stressed already we must bear in mind that in the Age of the Saints not only were the former Roman roads available for travel overland, but at the same time the western lands witnessed a marked revival of movement by sea. The Celtic saints made use of both methods of travel.

The implication of this analysis is that St. Padarn was more closely associated with what survived of Roman civilisation in South Wales than would appear to be the case with either St. Teilo or St. David. Paternus (the Latinized form of the saint's name) was a very common name in Roman times and several persons who bore it were honoured as saints in the Christian Church. Canon Doble thought that it was this fact that obscured the fame of the real Welsh St. Padarn, since it led to his ' Life ' being deliberately altered by a medieval hagiographer in order to identify him with another saint of the same name in Brittany, who had in turn already been confused with yet another Paternus.[1] The *Vita Paterni* is thus a collection of late and untrustworthy legends arranged by a writer who used the ' Lives ' of two other saints for his composition. Yet it is on this *Vita* that the supposed Breton origin of St. Padarn depends. Doble's work has shown very clearly that the Breton origin of St. Padarn can no longer be maintained and that it is necessary to search with Wade-Evans for a Letavia[2] in south-east Wales, not only as the home of St. Padarn but as the land of origin of a number of other important Welsh saints as well. We are inclined, therefore, to look for the cultural origins of St. Padarn in south-eastern Wales, emphasizing at the same time that he differed from so many of the early saints of these parts in that his sphere of influence lay in territories beyond the limits of the area itself, but, nevertheless, in regions closely

[1] G. H. Doble, *Saint Patern*, Cornish Saints' Series, No. 43, 1940, p. 1ff.

[2] The Latinized form of Llydaw (Eng. Brittany).

associated with the former Roman road-system. Such a view of St. Padarn may, in addition, be a pointer for those who believe that his activities preceded those of Dewi and Teilo.

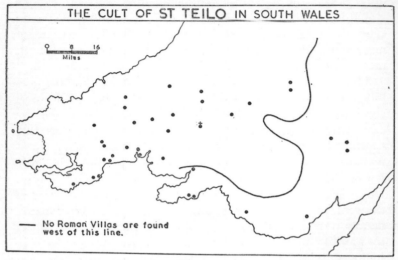

THE CULT OF ST TEILO IN SOUTH WALES

— No Roman Villas are found west of this line.

Fig. 15

If we possessed no ancient information whatsoever regarding St. Teilo and were forced to make an appraisal of his work based on the number and distribution of the churches dedicated to him, we would realise at once that he must be placed in a different category from that of St. Padarn. Many of his churches (see Fig. 15) lie beyond the zone of Roman influence, whether civil or military, in South Wales. They are most numerous in western Carmarthenshire and eastern Pembrokeshire, while his traditional *podum* was located at Llandeilo Fawr in the former county. It would appear that an extension of his cult took place eastwards both along the coastal route towards Kidwelly, Llandeilo Penybont, Gower, and Merthyr Mawr near Bridgend, and also along the well marked Roman road running eastward from near Llandovery into the Vale of Usk, for, just to the eastward of Abergavenny, we have a cluster of Teilo dedications at Llannarth, Llandeilo Gresynni and Llandeilo Porth Halog, all in Monmouthshire. Roman roads branching off to the northward from the main west to east route may have led to the foundation of Llandeilo'r fân in Brecknockshire and Llandeilo graban in Radnorshire. It is clear from the overall picture that the orientation of the distribution pattern is definitely west to east and not south to north as would appear to be the case with St. Padarn.

Another marked feature brought out by the distribution of the Teilo dedications is that they are clearly in keeping with a diffusion radiating from Llandeilo Fawr—the traditional centre of his cult—and not from Llandaf as the Norman protagonists of their newly created See in the twelfth century would have us believe in the *Liber Landavensis*. We are, however, fortunate in that we possess written evidence of the cult of St. Teilo reaching back at least three hundred years before the appearance of either the long and elaborate ' Life ' of the saint contained in the Book of Llandaf, or the recension of it now included in the British Museum Ms. Vesp. A.xiv. The early evidence is found in the famous gospel-book known as the Book of St. Chad now at Lichfield Cathedral. The gospels themselves would appear to have been written in Ireland before the year 700. Subsequently, they became the property of a church of St. Teilo, and while in its possession certain entries of considerable historical value were made in the margins of its pages. Sometime after 850 it passed into the possession of Lichfield Cathedral. The marginal entries are in Welsh and record gifts and agreements made ' on the altar of Teilo.' They tell us nothing about St. Teilo himself ; their significance lies in showing that even in the ninth century there was an active cult of the saint, and that the community in the monastery where the book was located was of the Celtic type governed by an abbot-bishop who called himself Bishop of St. Teilo. We are not told where this important monastery was, but an examination of the place names referred to in the Welsh entries makes it clear that it was at Llandeilo Fawr in Carmarthen-shire.[1]

The distribution of the Teilo churches presents a similar pattern to that formed by churches dedicated to St. David. It is this factor that tends to confirm the trad-itional view which stresses the close association between the two saints. The west Carmarthenshire and south-east Pembrokeshire group of Dewi churches is well marked, and so are those along the South Wales coastal plain towards Llangyfelach, the Gower peninsula and the Bridgend country, while equally clearly shown is the use of the Roman route from the upper Tywi valley to the Vale of Usk as represented by such settlements as Llywel, Y Trallwng, Llan-faes and Llanddew. The cult of the patron saint can be followed to the Monmouthshire section of the Usk, with churches in close proximity to those of St. Teilo at Capel David (near Abergavenny), Llanddewi Ysgyryd, Llanddewi Rhydderch and Rhaglan. There are also marked clusters of Dewi churches in the hills of northern Brecknockshire and in Radnorshire, and dedications to him are found even in western Herefordshire. Dedi-cations to St. Teilo, while decidedly less numerous than those to St. David, are, as we have seen, not unknown in the Brecknockshire region. It is, however, in western Pembrokeshire and in Cardiganshire, south of the Ystwyth-Wyre line, that Dewi dedications are numerous in areas where Teilo churches are unknown (see Fig. 16).

It is possible, and certainly in keeping with the traditional accounts, that it is in these western parts that we must seek both Dewi's birthplace and the centre of diffusion of his cult. Dewi churches are absent in the extreme north of Cardiganshire and it is not until we move southwards into the ancient commote of Anhuniog that they begin to

---

[1] G. H. Doble, *Saint Teilo*, Welsh Saints' Series, No. 3 (Lampeter, 1942), pp. 1-4. Canon Doble in this work suggests that St. Teilo may have been a disciple of St. Paulinus. This is of considerable interest in view of the proximity of Llandeilo Fawr to the area around Caeo and Llandovery where the cult of Paulinus seems to have been centred. Mr. R. D. Williams thinks that Dewi Sant was also a pupil of Paulinus at one stage removed. (*Y Llan*, Gorff. 18, 1952.)

appear. In this commote we find Henfynyw. This is where, according to Rhygyfarch's *Life of St. David*, written at Llanbadarn Fawr about 1090, the saint spent his boy-

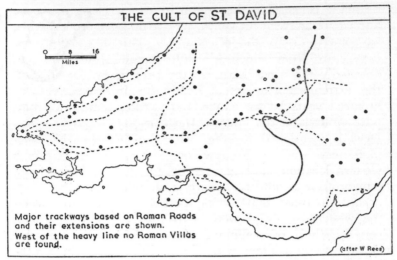

Fig. 16

hood. The parish church of Henfynyw is still dedicated to him with a Ffynnon Ddewi (David's Well) nearby. On this coast, too, are Llannon, named after his mother, and Llanina—the church of Dewi's reputed aunt, while still further southwards is Llangrannog, the monastery of St. Carannog, Dewi's uncle ; while scattered throughout the whole countryside from the Ystwyth-Wyre rivers in the north to the country south of the Teifi we have the foundations of his reputed cousins, Afan, Gwynlle, Pedr, Dogfael and Cenau.[1] Here we have another example of a feature so frequently found in Wales where saints who are linked closely together in the hagiological narrative appear to have foundations very close to each other on the ground. We have already indicated the view that it is most likely that the writers of the medieval ' Lives ' of the saints

---

[1] A. W. Wade-Evans, *The Life of St. David* (S.P.C.K., 1923). See Note 14, pp.84-5.

attempted to explain the topographical evidence by making saints commemorated in neighbouring dedications, brothers or cousins of their heroes. Whatever inference can now be made concerning the region in which Dewi was born and where he spent his youth, we are on safer ground when we come to discuss the location of his chief foundation and the centre from which his cult spread. This was undoubtedly the other Mynyw (the present St. David's) in the extreme north-west of Pembrokeshire. Nearly three hundred years before Rhygyfarch wrote, there was compiled in Ireland the famous *Martyrology of Oengus* in which Dewi is mentioned together with the fact that his chief monastery was at Mynyw or Menevia.[1] Its extreme western location must not be looked upon as the remote refuge of an anchorite. There is abundant evidence from prehistoric times that during periods such as this, when the western sea-ways were active, this peninsula was a veritable hub of communications. From this base St. David was in contact with Celtic Christianity in Southern Ireland, in south-western England and in Brittany, while along the various trackways that linked the western peninsula to what remained of the Roman roads, his cult was able to spread eastwards, as we have seen, over nearly the whole of South Wales (see Fig. 16). The resultant pattern formed by the distribution of Dewi churches in South Wales is what would be expected of such a western-based culture with links in southern Ireland and south-western England. Similarly based cultural distributions in prehistoric times likewise did not affect North Wales. Students of British pre-history now accept as axiomatic the fact that the cultures which affect North and South Wales respectively have entirely different origins. ' Throughout prehistoric times,' writes Sir Cyril Fox, ' there were strong forces tending to make North and South Wales separate entities.'[2] It is one of the basic contentions of this thesis that these prehistoric conditions survived the

[1] A. W. Wade-Evans, op. cit., p. vii.
[2] C. Fox, *The Personality of Britain*, 4th Edition (Cardiff, 1943), p. 73, Note 2.

Roman occupation of Wales and continued well into the Dark Ages. The exclusively southern provenance of the Dewi cult assumes a new significance against this background.

Recent work has shown that even the detail of the Dewi dedication-distribution pattern in South Wales can be matched in the archaeological field in the Dark Ages. Nash-Williams[1] has drawn attention to memorial stones of the early Christian period decorated with a simple cross and the Christian monograms I.H.S. and X.P.S., which he thinks exemplify a local type peculiar to Pembrokeshire. They occur in the St. David's area, mainly in the precincts of the Cathedral itself, and around nearby St. Edrens. Apart from the ones in the St. David's area a single (and possibly an early) example is found at Llanfeuno in Herefordshire. Llanfeuno lies within the Erging or Archenfield district which, as we have seen, was a stronghold of early Celtic Christianity and a seat of the cult of St. David. It is immaterial to the present argument that these monogram cross-slabs were almost certainly of Irish derivation; the point we wish to stress is that the St. David's peninsula and far-away western Herefordshire were in close cultural contact with one another in the Dark Ages, whether the culture be Archenfield or Irish in origin or just emanating from Tyddewi[2] itself.

It seems hardly necessary, therefore, to stress that the cult of St. David had reached the eastern borderlands of Wales long before the days of Rhygyfarch, and that its appearance there did not follow upon the publication of his *Life of St. David* after 1090. The dedications are, therefore, older than the hagiological literature we possess.

Bishop Asser, writing his Life of Alfred the Great circa 893, refers not only to the monastery of, but also to the *parochia* of, ' holy Degui ' as a well-known institution west of the river and north of the Severn Sea.[3] Recently, also,

---

[1] V. E. Nash-Williams, op. cit., p. 37.

[2] Lit. ' David's House '—the Welsh name for St. Davids.

[3] See W. H. Stevenson, *Asser's Life of King Alfred* (1904).

Sir Ifor Williams[1] has drawn attention to a possible interpretation of a line in the Welsh poem *Arymes Prydein Vawr* in the Book of Taliessin. He thinks that this poem had a South Wales origin and contends that the line in question should read that the author lived at Gelli-gaer.[2] This interpretation is important in so far as this poem contains several references to Dewi and although the actual manuscript is not earlier than the 13th century the material contained in the poem clearly belongs to an earlier date. Sir Ifor Williams thinks it represents an attempt to marshall under the fair banner of Dewi[3] the Breton, Cornish and Strathclyde Celts together with the Vikings of Dublin (all of whom are mentioned in the poem) in support of an anti-Hywel Dda party in South Wales, and in this way resist the growing power and influence of Aethelstan of England. If this contention is correct the poem can be dated between 927-931 when Aethelstan was exerting his power over the western kings.[4]   From the point of view of this chapter Sir Ifor Williams' conception of this poem would be yet another indication that the Dewi cult was active over the eastern part of South Wales a hundred and fifty years before the publication of Rhygyfarch's *Life*. The dedication distribution patterns are, therefore, older than the 'Lives' which were apparently written around them, and the narrative expanded by the addition of the usual tendentious material associated with hagiological literature.

The greatness of St. David as a South Wales saint is, therefore, beyond question and it seems clear that he had more in common with St. Teilo than with St. Padarn. The widespread distribution of his dedications may not be unrelated to the ancient tradition that he was a Dyfrwr —a Waterman (*Aquaticus*), the head and leader of the saints

---

[1] Gregynog Lectures delivered at the University College of Wales, Aberystwyth in 1950.

[2] ' poet tywyssawe dewi yr kynufwyr
Yn yr yggelli kaer am duw yssyd.'   18. 23-25.

[3] ' a lluman glan dewi a drychafant.'   16. 22.

[4] F. M. Stenton, *Anglo-Saxon England* (Oxford, 1943), pp. 336-7.

whom Gildas had occasion to praise[1]—in fact, the leader
of a puritan revival within the Celtic Church. As such,
St. David together with St. Teilo, might well be looked
upon as evangelists emerging from the remoter western
territories to denounce the broader faith of the south-
eastern zone.[2] Indeed, it may even be probable that we
have a remote echo of such a campaign preserved for us in
the dedication evidence itself. It is curious how many
churches are dedicated to either St. David or St. Teilo,
or both, while at the same time retaining traces of what
would appear to be earlier dedications. Three examples
chosen at random may be mentioned. The parish church
of Llangadog in Carmarthenshire, in spite of the clear
designation of the name, appears to have been dedicated
to St. David from very early times.[3] Some authorities
get over the anomaly by giving the dedication as to St.
David with St. Cadog.[4] Either dedication allows the
student to observe an interesting example of an original
Cadog foundation (significantly on the western fringe of
his cult) being taken over by the devotees of the later saint.
Llanarthne, also in the Tywi valley and now dedicated to
St. David, looks very much as if it originally belonged to
some lesser known saint and was later absorbed within
the cult of St. David. Similarly, at Llywel, situated on
the Roman road connecting the Vale of Tywi with the Usk
valley in Brecknockshire, Saints David and Teilo would
appear to have grafted themselves upon the local saint,
Llywel, as the church is at present dedicated to the three
saints together,[5] while the settlement significantly retains
St. Llywel's name. Whatever the precise missionary motive

[1] *Gildas* (Cymmrod. Record Series No. 3), pp. 160-161.

[2] E. G. Bowen, ' The Settlements of the Celtic Saints in South Wales',
Antiquity, Vol. XIX, 1945, p. 186.

[3] Roy. Comm. Ant. Mont. Wales, *Carmarthenshire*, Vol. 5, p. 429.

[4] Baring Gould and Fisher, *Lives of the British Saints*, Vol. II, p. 316.

[5] Baring-Gould and Fisher, *Lives of the British Saints*, Vol. III (1911), p. 387.
The statement in The Book of Llandaf (p. 275) that Hennlann Dibric and
Lann Teliau were ' in one cemetery ' at Hentland would, if correct, suggest
that even the Dubrician churches in Erging felt the force of the South-western
cults.

of St. David and his companions might have been, we are certain that the distribution of the Dewi churches determined to a very great extent the limits of the vast diocese of St. David's in the Middle Ages, in much the same way as the Dyfrig-Cadog-Illtud dedications determined the limits of the medieval diocese of Llandaf. The fact that Dewi dedications overlapped areas with Teilo dedications (see Fig. 16) helps to explain the boundary dispute which arose between the Bishops of Llandaf (claiming Teilo as the founder of their See) and St. David's when the two dioceses came to be delimited on a territorial basis after the Norman conquest.[1] What is, however, significant in the present context is that the territorial demarcation of the South Wales dioceses was in effect the consolidation of what had been two clearly marked cultural provinces in Early Christian times. We have already indicated that there is reason to believe that these areas were culturally distinct in Roman times and possibly throughout much of the prehistoric period as well.

We should note also that the fame of the great south-eastern monastic schools at Llanilltud Fawr and at Llan-carvan for classical as well as for Christian learning survived into Norman times and is clearly reflected in the work of the Norman hagiographers, while, on the contrary, no such traditions of ancient learning were ever associated with St. Teilo's *podum* at Llandeilo Fawr or with the Patron Saint's austere settlement in Glyn Rhosyn. Curiously (and, perhaps, significantly) Padarn's settlement at Llanbadarn Fawr seems to have retained traditions of learning more characteristic of the south-eastern monasteries, for Rhygyfarch himself was the son of Sulien the Wise whose family was renowned for its scholastic and artistic attainments. Their work can still be gauged by a small group of manuscripts dispersed between Cambridge, London and Dublin. What is of particular interest in the present context is that long before the time of Rhygyfarch something had happened to the fortunes of Llanbadarn Fawr. Rhygyfarch's own

[1] William Rees, *An Historical Atlas of Wales* (Cardiff, 1951), p. 23.

brother Ieuan, in his well-known poem about his father
Sulien, shows a wistful remembrance of the former greatness
of the monastery.[1] There had been here the nucleus of
what could have become a territorial bishopric (including
most of Cardiganshire and Radnorshire where the Padarn
dedications are found), yet all this territory had clearly
been absorbed into the sphere of influence of St. David
long before Rhygyfarch's time, and we have the spectacle
of St. David's own ' Life ' being written by ' a son to St.
Padarn.' May it not be that here again, and on a scale
greater than previously indicated, we have the cult of a
pre-Davidic saint, with possible Romano-British leanings,
being drawn within the orbit of Dewi Ddyfrwr.

It is not within the purview of this chapter to discuss the
extent to which Dewi's influence, or that of any other saint
mentioned here, spread across the seas. It is possible,
judging by dedication evidence, that St. David may have
laboured in Southern Ireland, and that he and St. Teilo
may have worked in Cornwall and in Brittany. It is
possible, too, that daughter establishments of their monasteries, perhaps even whole communities surrounding them,
forced for some reason to leave Wales, may have carried
the cults of their patrons overseas at a later (but still early)
period. Such communities may have taken with them
the names of the places from which they came and given
them to their new homes. In any case, the links between
the southern portions of Celtic Europe in the days of Dewi
and Teilo are as clear and as unmistakable as they appear
to have been on numerous previous occasions during the
long interval that separated the Age of the Saints from the
far-off days of the Megalith builders.

[1] Quoted by Doble in *Saint Patern*, op. cit., p. 8.

CHAPTER IV

THE NORTHERN CULTS

THERE is abundant evidence that the Irish Sea throughout prehistoric times tended to be the centre of a vast cultural province frequently uniting its much fractionated and indented coastlands under a single cultural stimulus. That the Irish Sea continued to perform this function in post-Roman times is clearly seen in the Age of the Saints. North Wales occupies a central position in this vast province and throughout pre-historic times it was distinguished, not as a creative centre in art or craftsmanship but, on the contrary, stood out by virtue of its acquisitions. It can be shown to have been accessible to travellers and merchants from at least three major routes across the sea ; from Ireland in the west ; from Strathclyde, Galloway and Cumbria in the north ; and from South Wales, Cornwall and western France in the south. In addition, there was a clearly marked land-route across the mountains from the bend of the Severn near Shrewsbury on to the Berwyn range and thence over the Dee, south of Corwen and westward to the Conway, and so across the Snowdon country to the Menai Straits. This route linked North Wales not only with the lower and middle Severn valley, but also with southern and eastern Britain generally.[1] On occasions, archaeologists have emphasized the dual character of the Irish Basin in the cultural sense, stressing the existence of a northern and a southern sub-province. Even when such a division is clearly marked it is characteristic of North Wales (in virtue of its central position) to share the characteristics of both provinces. It is there-

---

[1] Sir Cyril Fox has demonstrated how some of these routes must have been used in assembling the spectacular Iron Age material found at Llyn Cerrig Bach in Anglesey in 1943 (see C. Fox, *A Find of the Early Iron Age from Llyn Cerrig Bach, Anglesey* (Nat. Mus. of Wales : Cardiff, 1946, especially pp. 59 ff.).

fore against this background that we must approach the dedication-distribution patterns in the North. Before doing so, it is possible to discuss a little further the four approaches we have named with particular reference to their relative importance in the Dark Ages.

As the Anglo-Saxon conquest spread over Lowland Britain contacts between North Wales and southern and eastern England ceased, and the function of the land-route across the mountains was confined to linking the sea-plain of north-west Wales with the middle and southern Border-land. Travellers in the Dark Ages would also tend to use what remained of the Roman military roads in the partly cleared valley bottoms in preference to the former pre-historic trackway which clung to the middle slopes of the hills. Thus, as far as North Wales was concerned the sea-routes grew in importance as compared with the land routes. Developments along the sea-routes were by no means uniform, for it is clear that the Celtic Church in Ireland was more closely linked with southern, than with northern, Wales throughout this period. It is worth recalling in this context the evidence of the Ogham inscribed stones discussed in Chapter I, for they demonstrate very clearly the strength of the Irish connections with South Wales at this time. Equally important is the evidence marshalled by Sir Cyril Fox and Mr. H. A. Hyde to show that even from about 500 B.C. onwards such trade as existed between Ireland and Britain made use of the southern, or Bristol Channel, route.[1] Thus, we shall find that North Wales owed much more to the Celtic saints who arrived by sea from the north and south, and to those who followed the Roman roads from the eastward, than it did to the few who reached its shores from the west.

It is important in developing our main thesis to begin with the southern sea-route. From this direction Christianity from Western Gaul appears to have established itself very early in North Wales. In his survey of the Early Christian monuments the late Dr. Nash-Williams pointed out

---

[1] C. Fox and H. A. Hyde, *Antiq. Journ.* 1939, p. 382 ff.

that of the six earliest examples found in Wales (with their inscriptions arranged in horizontal lines in the classical Roman fashion) four occur in North Wales ; two in Caernarvonshire, at Bodafan and Penmachno, the third near Barmouth, and the fourth at Llanerfyl in Montgomeryshire.[1] We have already followed up the implications of this distribution by drawing attention to what we presume to be dedications to very early Celtic saints in North Wales —members of the traditional family of Maxen Wledig.[2] Such dedications are confined, like the majority of the Early Christian inscribed stones, to the western half of North Wales (see Fig. 2).

It was along the same seaways from the South that either St. Illtud himself, or one of his immediate followers, established a cell at Llanelltud in western Merionethshire, while St. Cadog, likewise, touched upon the north-east coast of Anglesey (where there was formerly a chapel dedicated to him in the parish of Amlwch) presumably on his way to Clydeside where the ancient church of Cambuslang is dedicated to him. In this way the coastal fringes of North Wales would appear to have some contact, however slight, with the early Romano-Celtic Christianity of south-eastern Wales. It is possible that the saints culted at Llansadwrn and Llangwnnadl, in Anglesey and Caernarvonshire respectively, represent still further evidence of early southern contacts with the North by sea. The names of both saints Saturninus (Sadwrn) and Vendesetl (Gwynhoedl) appear on early inscribed stones in North Wales. Sadwrn is said, in late and often untrustworthy sources, to be a brother of St. Illtud. It is possible, however, that this may be correct, both in view of the occurrence of Sadwrn's name in an early sixth century context and the fact that he has links with South Wales at Llansadwrn in Carmarthenshire. The name Vendesetl occurs again in a variant spelling on an inscribed stone associated with the prominent hill-top church of Llan-saint, in the same county,

---

[1] V. E. Nash-Williams, op. cit., Nos. 83, 101, 271 and 294.
[2] See Chapter I, p.22.

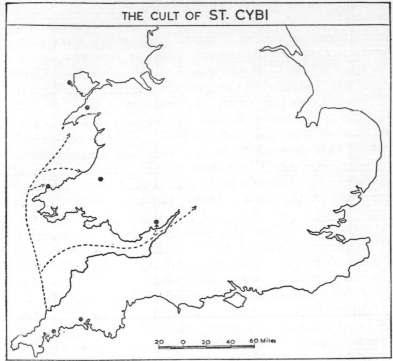

Fig. 17

which overlooks Carmarthen Bay.[1]

However tenuous our evidence may be for the part played by the southern sea-routes in the early Christianization of the North, their significance at a later period is abundantly clear. One example must suffice. The Cornish saint Cubi (Cybi) has two churches dedicated to him in his native territory, namely Cuby and Tregony, although Landulph between the rivers Tamar and Lynher seems also to have been his.[2] In his journeys northwards he appears to have visited the eastern portion of the Bristol Channel as we have an important dedication to him at Llangibby-on-Usk

[1] Roy. Comm. Anc. Mont. *Carmarthenshire*, Vol. 5, No. 719.
[2] G H. Doble, *Saint Cubi (Cybi)*; *A Celtic Saint*, Cornish Saints' Series, No. 22.

F

in south-eastern Wales. The occurrence of an islet called Ynys Gybi off the Pen-caer peninsula of Pembrokeshire and the presence of another Llangybi in the valley of the westward flowing Teifi suggests the use of the west Wales coast in approaching Llŷn and Anglesey, where we have Llangybi, near Pwllheli, and Caergybi which is Holyhead. (Fig. 17)

We can now turn to the northern route. W. F. Grimes in attempting to sum up the cultural position of Wales in prehistoric times has stated that ' . . . the north coastal plain looks naturally towards Yorkshire and Northern England generally.'[1] No student can overlook the significance of this statement in the Age of the Saints. It would appear from the works of Hemp, Gresham, Bersu, Griffiths and Hogg on the hut circles in north-west Wales and elsewhere, that there were extensive movements of people from northern England and southern Scotland into North Wales taking place at intervals from the second century B.C. to the seventh century of the Christian era.[2] Those that took place during, and immediately following, the Roman occupation were obviously associated with the well-known Roman policy of transferring *Foederati* to a district where restless native tribes were likely to prove troublesome. It was the application of this scheme to Gwynedd, sometime towards the close of the Roman period that accounts for the well-known invasion of North Wales by the ' Sons of Cunedda.' Collingwood[3] suggests that this transference was

---

[1] W. F. Grimes, *Guide to the Collection illustrating the Prehistory of Wales* (National Museum of Wales : Cardiff, 1939), p. 110.

[2] See among other references, W. J. Hemp and C. A. Gresham, ' Hut Circles in North Wales', *Antiquity*, XVIII, 1944, pp. 183-196 ; G. Bersu and W. E. Griffiths, ' Concentric Circles at Llwyn-du Bach, Penygroes, Caernarvonshire', *Arch. Camb.*, 1949, pp. 173-204 and A. H. A. Hogg, ' The Votadini ' in *Aspects of Archaeology in Britain and Beyond* presented to O. G. S. Crawford, London, 1951, pp. 200-220. Hut groups in Anglesey were clearly in use as late as the 6th century A.D. for, at Pant-y-Saer in the parish of Llanfair Mathafarn Eithaf, a silver penannular brooch has been found similar to Scottish examples of the sixth century. The find is of considerable importance in showing the links between southern Scotland and North Wales at this time. (C. W. Phillips, ' Excavation of a Hut Group at Pant-y-Saer, Anglesey,' *Arch. Camb.* LXXXIX 1934, pp. 18-20).

[3] R. G. Collingwood and J. N. L. Myres, *Roman Britain and the English Settlements*, 1941 Edition, p. 289.

the work of Stilicho at the end of the fourth century forming part of his scheme for the reorganization of the northern frontier of Britain, and that the Votadini—the centre of whose territory was in the neighbourhood of North Berwick —were mainly involved. This suggestion in its major outlines has received interesting confirmation in recent times on linguistic grounds by Professor Sir Ifor Williams[1] and on archaeological grounds by the work of Bersu and Griffiths.[2]

Hemp and Gresham dealing with the unenclosed hut-groups in north-west Wales in their 1944 paper produce cogent arguments for believing that their builders were intruders who arrived by sea from the North at some time between the first or second century B.C. and the Dark Ages. The concentric hut-circles of the Dark Ages described by Bersu and Griffiths and associated by Ralegh Radford with the followers of Cunedda,[3] are found in much the same positions as the unenclosed groups. We are, therefore, fully justified in deriving the Cunedda invasion, in like manner, by sea from the North. Controversy, however, remains concerning the precise date of this movement. Hunter Blair[4] followed by Charlesworth favours a date round about 450 A.D., while Hogg[5] argues in favour of the period slightly before 400 A.D.

We have made this rather lengthy digression into the current views concerning the Cunedda invasion because it is essential to understand it aright if we are to proceed to a study of the numerous churches in North Wales dedicated to saints who followed in its wake—many of whom, tradition claims, were descendants of Cunedda himself.

If we adopt the Hunter Blair-Charlesworth chronology it is possible to believe that Cunedda and his sons were at

[1] Sir Ifor Williams, *Canu Aneirin* (Caerdydd, 1938), pp. i-xciii.
[2] Bersu and Griffiths, op. cit., pp. 173-204.
[3] C. A. Ralegh Radford, ' Llwyn-du Bach and Early Welsh Society', Appendix II to Bersu and Griffiths, op. cit., pp. 205-6.
[4] P. Hunter Blair, ' The Origins of Northumbria', *Arch. Aeliana*, Series 4, Vol. XXV (1947), pp. 1-51.
[5] A. H. A. Hogg, ' The Date of Cunedda', *Antiquity* XXII, 1948, pp. 201-205.

least nominally Christians before their movement into North Wales, for there exists strong archaeological evidence for the Christianization of the Scottish Lowlands south of the Forth-Clyde line following upon the mission of St. Ninian in the fourth century.[1] His work would appear to form part of the same Gallo-Roman missionary activity that affected Wales about the same time. This would add weight to Charlesworth's useful suggestion that the Votadini had been made *Foederati* under Magnus Maximus, in the days of Cunedda's grandfather, and as *Foederati* they had been moved to protect British territory against Irish raiders on the orders of St. Germanus during his second visit in 447 A.D.[2]

Fig. 18 shows the location of churches, chapels and other sacred sites bearing the names of saints said to be descendants of Cunedda through Einion Yrth to the sixth generation. Saints Einion Frenhin, Seiriol, Meirion, Eurgain and Edern are included in this genealogy. The concentration of these dedications in north-west Wales is significant, as this is the area into which the original entry is presumed to have been effected if the object was to deal with Irish settlers in these parts.

As later saints came from the Celtic North to settle among their kinsmen in Wales,[3] the resultant dedication-distribution takes on a new form. If we examine the traditional genealogy of a reputed Northern chieftain, Coel Godebog, and plot the churches dedicated to all the saints mentioned among his descendants to the ninth generation,[4] (see Fig. 19), we observe that the map now indicates not only a Gwynedd concentration but, in addition, another in Flint and eastern Denbighshire, not to mention the scattered

[1] See a review by O. G. S. Crawford of Hunter Blair, 'The Origins of Northumbria', in *Antiquity* XXII, 1948, pp. 51-52.

[2] M. P. Charlesworth, *The Lost Province* (Cardiff, 1949), pp. 27-39.

[3] It is clear from the 'Book of Aneirin' that the Votadini were still extant as a tribe in the North in the VI century A.D. (See Sir Ifor Williams, op. cit., pp. i-xciii).

[4] The following well-known North Wales saints, among others, are included in this list : Asaph, Cenau, Collen, Cynfarch, Cynwyl, Deiniol, Deiniolen, Dunawd, Grwst, Gwynnin, Maethlu, Nidan and Pabo Post Prydyn.

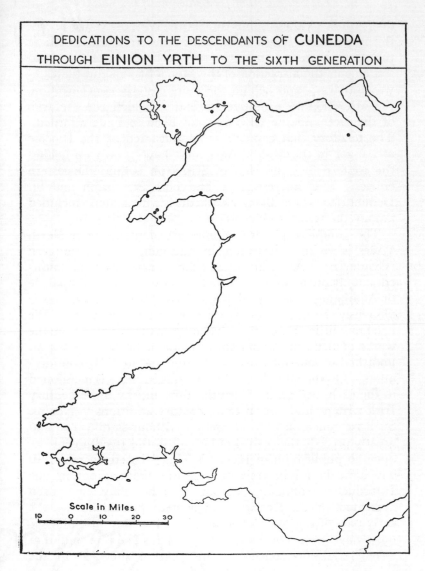

DEDICATIONS TO THE DESCENDANTS OF **CUNEDDA**
THROUGH **EINION YRTH** TO THE SIXTH GENERATION

Scale in Miles

Fig. 18

dedications to these saints in South Wales. If we accept the importance of sea communications from the North at this time, then it is tempting to see behind the Gwynedd settlements the attraction of the Menai Straits and the Conway estuary ; and behind the more easterly concentration, the attraction to primitive navigators which the estuaries of the Dee and the Clwyd must likewise have afforded.[1] The territory that came to be administered as the Diocese of Bangor in the Middle Ages must have grown up behind the western foci and that of St. Asaph behind the eastern entries. It is interesting to find both St. Asaph and St. Deiniol (to whom Bangor cathedral is dedicated) included among the reputed descendants of Coel Godebog.

The complete picture of northern contacts with North Wales is vividly illustrated by the cult of St. Kentigern (Cyndeyrn). As an historical character he has been doubted, largely owing to the fact that he is not mentioned by Bede or Adamnan, and that his ' Life ' by Jocelyn of Furness is obviously late, and of a very legendary character. We need pay little attention to the omission of his name from the works of Bede or Adamnan, as to them he belonged to an unorthodox and inferior ' race ' and merited no consideration. On the other hand, however, Kentigern is mentioned in the early pedigrees of British saints and by ninth century Irish writers, and also in tenth century additions to Nenius. Such references are not altogether without significance and greatly precede the revival of his cult in the twelfth century, and the publication of Jocelyn's ' Life ' based on materials which he found in Ireland. As was pointed out in the Introduction[2] although certain churches may have been dedicated to St. Kentigern in western Britain during the early part of the twelfth century, it is clear that his influence must have been considerable during his lifetime and that a real tradition concerning his mission survived in the

[1] The Mersey estuary offers yet another easy entry inland and must have been equally attractive (see Fig. 20 inset), but all evidence of Celtic dedications has been obliterated by strong English administration since the seventh century.

[2] See p. 8.

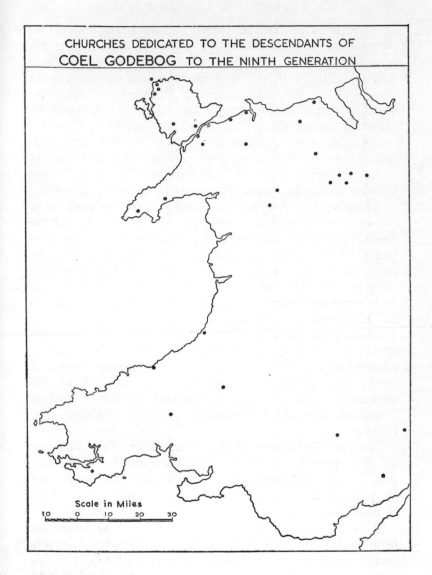

CHURCHES DEDICATED TO THE DESCENDANTS OF
COEL GODEBOG TO THE NINTH GENERATION

Scale in Miles

Fig. 19

areas wherein he had laboured. There is nothing in the distribution pattern shown on Fig. 20 (which attempts to mark churches dedicated to him and to his immediate followers) that is in any way incompatible with the broad outline of the legends concerning St. Kentigern that survived into the Middle Ages. His ' Life ' relates how he laboured among the northern Britons and then, when an anti-Christian party came into power, he left the North and sought refuge among his kinsmen who had already come to North Wales as followers of Cunedda. While Cyndeyrn was in North Wales we hear of the founding of Llanelwy (St. Asaph), and finally when the position in Strathclyde swung once again in the saint's favour he returned thither, taking with him, it is thought, some of his North Wales followers. On his return to Scotland the range of his missionary work was extended and we find churches dedicated to him in the east Grampian valleys. It is significant that associated with these dedications to St. Kentigern in Mar are others to St. Nidan and St. Ffinnan, presumably two of his North Wales disciples who also have churches dedicated to them almost side by side— Llanfinnan and Llanidan—near to the Anglesey shores of the Menai. In this way we see that Cyndeyrn had cultural associations with both the eastern and the western foci of ' northern derived ' Christianity in North Wales.[1] (See Fig. 20).

The full significance of the distribution of this cult can not be appreciated without reference to the interesting parallels that exist between the distribution patterns formed by plotting the sites on which certain prehistoric objects of northern origin have been found.

It would appear, for example, that during the Late Bronze Age there were extensive movements of people from northern Britain into the coastlands bordering the Irish Sea at a time when new and large invasions were taking

---

[1] E. G. Bowen, ' The Saints of Gwynedd', *Trans. Caern. Hist. Socy.*, 1948, pp. 3-4.

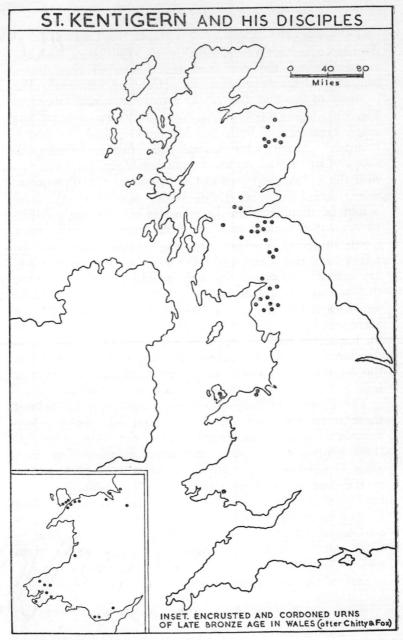

ST. KENTIGERN AND HIS DISCIPLES

INSET. ENCRUSTED AND CORDONED URNS
OF LATE BRONZE AGE IN WALES (after Chitty & Fox)

Fig. 20

place across the Narrow Seas into Lowland Britain.[1] Archaeologists are agreed that the distribution of both the encrusted and the cordoned burial-urns of this period indicate such movements in Highland Britain. The location of the find-sites of these urns in Wales (see inset Fig. 20), shows clearly that these southern moving folk made great use of both the Mersey-Dee and the Menai ' entries.' Those who moved still further southwards followed the coastal routes, for pottery of this kind is found near the western seaboard of Cardiganshire ; in Pembrokeshire, and along the South Wales sea-plain. While it would be manifestly unwise to stress too far the parallels between distributions resulting from large scale folk-movements involving Scotland, Ireland, northern England, the Isle of Man and Wales, and those resulting from the missionary activities of one individual (possibly involving church dedications established many generations after the initial activities of the saint), nevertheless, it is important for the argument in this book to note that the close association of St. Kentigern and his followers with the lands adjacent to the two North Wales ' entries ' is yet a further example of the survival of conditions that were apparently in being at least a thousand years before the days of the Saints.

The dioceses of Bangor and St. Asaph grew up behind these respective ' foci ' in later times, but, before their consolidation in the territorial sense in the Norman period, there existed, naturally, a close association between these areas of northern immigration. This is already apparent in the case of St. Kentigern, while other examples come readily to mind. The same St. Deiniol who established Bangor in Arfon established also Bangor-is-coed (Bangor-on-Dee) together with two of its ancient chapels—Marchwiail and Worthenbury—which are likewise dedicated to him.[2] An example in the opposite direction, as it were, is that of the Powysian saint, Tysilio. The centre of his

---

[1] C. Fox, ' An Encrusted Urn of the Bronze Age', *Antiquaries Journal*, VII 1927, p. 115.

[2] J. E. Lloyd, *A History of Wales*, Vol. I (3rd Edition, 1939), p. 193.

cult was at Meifod in Montgomeryshire. He is the patron
of Llandysilio in that county, as well as of Llandysilio-yn-
Iâl and Bryn Eglwys in Denbighshire. In addition to
these Powysian dedications we find St. Tysilio culted at
Llandysilio in Anglesey on the northern shores of the
Menai Straits. The location of this dedication together
with another in south-western Cardiganshire and a further
one on the borders of Pembrokeshire and Carmarthenshire
strongly suggests that St. Tysilio besides being a local saint
of Powys had on some occasion, like so many of his contemporaries, journeyed along the thalassic route (see Fig.
21).

Contacts between the eastern and western cultural
provinces of North Wales in the Age of the Saints, are,
however, best demonstrated by the widespread cult of St.
Beuno. The numerous dedications to this saint show
clearly that he must have made considerable use of what
remained of the Roman road system in North Wales.
(See Figs. 22 and 23). This brings us to a consideration
of the third and last of the three important means of access
to North Wales mentioned at the beginning of this chapter.

As we have seen from the archaeological evidence there
were at least some Gallo-Roman Christians in north-east
Wales in the early phases of the ' Western ' Christianization
of the country. Nash-Williams records early Christian
inscribed stones belonging to his Group I at Llanerfyl in
Montgomeryshire, Clocaenog in Denbighshire and Caerwys in Flintshire. The epigraphical evidence indicates
that the Llanerfyl and Clocaenog stones belong to the
late fifth or early sixth century, the former indicating very
early features, while the latter is, significantly, one of the
very few Ogham inscribed stones in North Wales. Both
are undoubtedly earlier than the Caerwys stone.[1] Dedication distributions indicate that the territories in which
these three stones are found became very active centres of
Celtic Christianity in later times. It should be remembered
that the higher relief of North Wales allowed fewer west-

[1] V. E. Nash-Williams, op. cit., Nos. 176, 184 and 294.

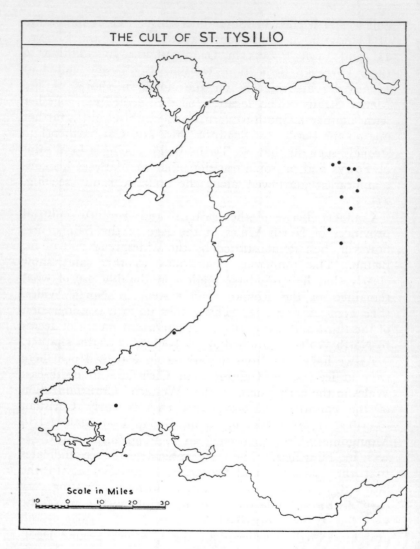

THE CULT OF ST. TYSILIO

Scale in Miles

Fig. 21

east transmontane routes in Roman times as compared with South Wales. In the North the main arteries would appear to run from south to north on either side of the mountain mass. Thus, the only possible parallel for the Llandovery-Brecon-Abergavenny transverse route in the North would be the Bala-cleft route, linking the fort at Caergai with that at Ffrith ; but even this cannot be traced with accuracy across the Merionethshire mountains to the west coast. Even so, when the Gallo-Roman Christians, arriving on our western shores, did manage to penetrate eastwards in North Wales they found before them a much less Romanized country than their comrades discovered in South-eastern Wales. The absence of Roman villas in eastern Wales north of the Severn is a clearly marked feature of the map of Roman Britain.[1] The contrast between North and South Wales in this respect is reflected in the absence of great *scholastic* monasteries comparable with Llancarfan and Llanilltud Fawr in the South. Likewise, there are no indigenous saints in the north-east comparable in importance and antiquity to Saints Dyfrig, Cadog and Illtud. The only possible exception is the Powysian saint Beuno, but all the circumstantial evidence we possess suggests that he comes very late into the story and that even in his case there survived into the Middle Ages a persistent tradition that he received his education in the south-east. We have no knowledge of where the original ' Life ' of St. Beuno was written. All we know is that the Welsh version prepared by the anchorite of Llanddewi-brefi in Cardiganshire in the fourteenth century is an abbreviated translation or paraphrase, or both, of some lost Latin *Vita* of the saint and thus certainly embodies traditions older than the first half of the fourteenth century.[2] What is significant, however, is that there is nothing in the distribution pattern formed by the churches known to be dedicated to St. Beuno (see Fig. 22) which is inconsistent with the traditions which survived into the Middle Ages

[1] Ordnance Survey Map of Roman Britain, 1928.
[2] A. W. Wade-Evans, ' Beuno Sant', *Arch. Camb.*, 1930, pp. 315 ff.

concerning the field of his labours. He has churches
dedicated to him in four regions of eastern Wales.   His
most southerly church is at Llanfeuno under Clodock in
south-western Herefordshire, situated close to the Roman
road that linked Gobannium to Kenchester—a memorial,

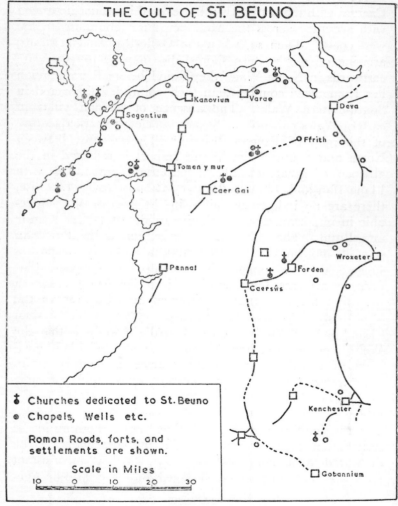

Fig. 22

possibly, of St. Beuno's contacts with south-eastern Wales. The other areas where the Beuno cult is found in eastern Wales are closely related to the three outposts of Gallo-Roman Christianity to which reference has already been made. There are Berriew and Betws Cedewain in eastern Montgomeryshire, not far from Llanerfyl, and situated along a well-marked strip of Roman road linking the fort at Caersŵs to that at Forden. In this district Beuno is said to have been born—the descendant of a princely family. Mathrafal, the seat of the early kings of Powys, is also in the same territory. Further north we have Gwyddelwern dedicated to St. Beuno. Nearby is his holy well, with another bearing his name at Betws Gwerful Goch. Gwyddelwern is alongside the Roman road running between Caer Gai and Ffrith, while the Clocaenog stone is not far away. In the extreme north-east, Whitford church was originally dedicated to St. Beuno and he possesses an ancient chapel at Llanasa, and a holy well in Tremeirchion parish and another at Holywell itself. All these sites are closely associated with Roman remains in Flintshire and in a similar context we find the sixth century Christian inscribed stone at Caerwys.

The next largest concentration of Beuno dedications is to be found in the Gwynedd country of the north-west. The churches at Aberffraw and Trefdraeth in south-western Anglesey, together with Clynnog Fawr, Pistyll, Carnguwch and Botwnnog in Llŷn are dedicated to him and there is abundant evidence of his cult in their vicinity. Exactly how this Venedotian group of churches was linked with the Powysian one is not known, but the use of the former Roman road system is indicated. The presence of Beuno dedications at Llanycil (complete with holy well) near to the Roman fort of Caer-gai in Merioneth and again at Penmorfa (also with a holy well and in a sub-Roman context) about three miles off the Tomen-y-Mur—Segontium road may present a clue as to the route followed (see Fig. 22). At any rate, there is considerably more map evidence to show that St. Beuno in the sixth century was following what remained of the Roman roads to get from Powys to north-west Wales than there is to suggest that he followed the pre-historic trackway over the mountains that Sir Cyril Fox has traced so clearly from the bend of the Severn near Shrewsbury on to the Menai Straits.[1]

We can not leave the cult of St. Beuno without adding two further comments. The first relates to the close correspondence between the hagiological and the topographical evidence concerning the saint, and the second to the similarities, however strained, that appear to exist between his mission in North Wales and that of St. David in South Wales.

The ' Life ' of St. Beuno mentions that during his peregrinations he gathered around him a band of followers who are distinctly named, and if we plot the sites of the churches still dedicated to these individuals (as is attempted on Fig. 23) we are immediately impressed by the close relationship they bear geographically to the churches dedicated to St. Beuno himself. In the neighbourhood of Berriew and Betws Cedewain we have Guilsfield, dedicated to St. Aelhaearn ;   Llanengan and Llanwyddelan, dedicated to Llorcan Wyddel ;   and Llanllwchaearn and Llamyrewig both dedicated to Llwchaearn. These three saints are frequently mentioned in the *Vita*. Similarly, near Gwyddelwern, St. Aelhaearn had a chapel in former times which is now extinct, while not far away is Llangwyfan, dedicated to St. Cwyfan, another of St. Beuno's followers. In the Whitford area of Flintshire the Beuno dedications are closely associated with those of St. Winifred. In Llŷn and Anglesey, the same feature is shown. Saints Aelhaearn, Cwyfan, Edern, Deiniol Fab and Twrog, all of whom are mentioned in the *Vita*, have dedications in Llŷn and Arfon close to the Beuno churches, while Cwyfan, Deiniol Fab, Dona, Ceidio, Edern and Twrog appear again in Anglesey where St. Beuno has several important dedications. The significance of this correlation between the hagiological and the topographical evidence has

[1] See page 66.

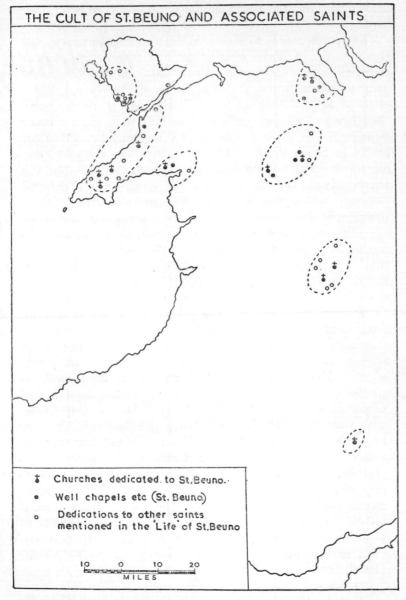

THE CULT OF ST. BEUNO AND ASSOCIATED SAINTS

☩   Churches dedicated to St. Beuno.

●   Well chapels etc (St. Beuno)

○   Dedications to other saints
      mentioned in the 'Life' of St. Beuno

10   0   10   20

MILES

G   Fig. 23

already been mentioned in Chapter I and needs no re-iteration here.[1]

That St. Beuno is in North Wales the counterpart of St. David in South Wales rests in the first place on numerical evidence alone. Although the total number of Beuno dedications in North Wales amounts to barely a quarter of those to St. David in South Wales, yet there are more churches and chapels dedicated to him than to any other saint in North Wales. The same thing may be said of St. David in South Wales. The similarity does not end here, for much in the same way as it would appear that the Patron Saint led a mission from the south-western cultural province which finally spread into south-eastern Wales ; likewise, St. Beuno seems to have led a mission in the opposite direction, from Powys into north-west Wales—into territory untouched by St. David. We have already shown that it is unlikely that Beuno belonged to the Romano-British school of Saints Dyfrig, Cadog and Illtud and there is no echo of such a suggestion in his ' Life '; his missionary zeal is more like that of Dewi Sant. It is even possible that he might have been a contemporary of the Patron Saint, or possibly followed him a generation later. In any case, Beuno's settlement at Llanfeuno in south-western Herefordshire is significant for it is located, as we have seen, in a region which on archaeological and hagiological evidence is known to have been closely linked with distant St. David's for many generations.[2] It may be, then, that the cults were linked ; representing together a late phase in the spread of Celtic Christianity—Beuno carrying the Dewi asceticism over North Wales. Whatever our views may be, it is at least curious that a fourteenth century anchorite in one of Dewi's most famous cells in South Wales should have thought it worthwhile to re-write the ' Life ' of this otherwise exclusively northern saint in the same book as he re-wrote the ' Life ' of St. David.

[1] See page 30.
[2] See p. 61.   There are four Dewi churches in this area—Much Dewchurch, Little Dewchurch, Dewsall and Kilpeck, all within a few miles of Llanfeuno.

CHAPTER V

PEREGRINI

THE title of this chapter needs a little explanation. In a general sense almost all the Celtic saints were *peregrini* and so it might be considered that the title is more appropriate for the book as a whole than for a single chapter within it. Nevertheless, it is clear that as the western sea-routes entered on a period of ever increasing activity as the barbarian invasions of south-eastern England grew in intensity, large numbers of itinerant saints either left the shores of Wales for other lands or arrived on her coasts by sea. Dedications to these late saints are likely to be more sporadic than those to earlier saints upon whose dedication-distribution patterns the south-eastern, south-western and northern culture areas have been based. This alone would appear to be a valid reason for giving the *peregrini* separate consideration.

The location of sites dedicated to these saints indicates that they reached Wales by sea, either singly, or in groups from the Celtic North, from Ireland in the west, and from Cornwall and possibly Brittany in the south ; while others certainly left Wales for these destinations. This chapter will direct attention primarily to the *peregrini* using the southern and western routes, for those from the north have already been discussed in Chapter IV.

Doble has shown that a group of saints commemorated in the New Quay—Padstow—Bodmin area of mid-Cornwall are all in some way connected with each other. They are Saints Petroc, Congar, Cadoc, Mawgan, Hernin, Carantoc, Gwbert, Brioc and Collen.[1] Their provenance is, however, not confined to Cornwall. There are churches dedicated to all of them in Wales, and to most of them in Brittany, while four are also honoured in Somerset (Fig.

[1] G. H. Doble, *St. Carantoc* and *St. Brioc* in the Cornish Saints Series, Nos. 14 and 17 respectively.

24). These saints, or their cults, seem to have originated in Wales and to have spread across the Channel to Cornwall where we find their churches in the hinterland of the northward facing tidal estuaries of the Gamel and the Camel. From here they, or their followers, passed across the trans-peninsular route to the Fowey and so by sea to Brittany. The Somerset dedications suggest that some of the saints may have taken the shorter crossing further up the Bristol channel and then spread along the coast to Cornwall. It is a well known fact that throughout pre-historic times the shorter upper crossings were used when Lowland Britain was free from continental invasions, but at periods when south-eastern Britain was disturbed and the sea-routes of the west entered upon a period of greater activity, then the outer, as well as the inner, crossings of the Bristol Channel came into use.[1] The above evidence suggests that such conditions survived into the Dark Ages.

Once more we must take note of the fact that medieval hagiologists made those saints who had churches dedicated to them in close proximity to each other into brothers, companions or pupils of their particular heroes. We have sought to show, for example, in earlier chapters that St. Cadog was one of the pioneers of Christian Wales. He might have lived almost two hundred years before the *peregrini* we are now considering, yet in the medieval ' Life ' of St. Cadog, St. Petroc (owing to the geographical proximity of some of his churches to those of St. Cadog) is introduced into the story as Cadog's uncle, and it is likely for a similar reason that the holy man Moucan or Maucan, mentioned in the ' Life ' as intervening to obtain reconciliation between St. Cadog and Maelgwn Gwynedd, may be the St. Mawgan referred to above.[2] The geographical proximity of these and other dedications may be evidence that the dedications themselves are older than the ' Lives ' of the saints, but constitutes no evidence that all these

---

[1] R. M. Prothero, ' Bristol Channel Coastlands : Early Cultural Contacts', *Scot. Geog. Mag.* Vol. 65, 1949, pp. 44-54.

[2] Baring Gould and Fisher, *Lives of the British Saints*, III, p. 481.

saints were contemporaries, or used the sea-routes of the west at the same time, or that they necessarily moved in the same direction. All that we are certain of is that these men, or some of their followers desirous of honouring their names, did use the sea-routes of western Britain in the Dark Ages to propagate their cults. We need not, therefore, at this juncture be involved in any further treatment of the cult of St. Cadog in Wales, and so his numerous dedications have been omitted from the Welsh area in Fig. 24. His association with the group of saints we are now considering is clearly anomalous in that we find that most Welsh saints culted in Cornwall or Brittany usually have little or no cult in the country of their origin,[1] and such is obviously not the case with St. Cadog.

The distribution of dedications to the remaining members of this group in Wales itself is generally sporadic, but there is, nevertheless, a clearly marked tendency towards a choice of site within easy access of the coast. This is clearly seen by the number of sites which lie within the limits of the natural drainage flowing northwards, westwards and southwards to the Welsh coast (see Fig. 24).[2] The most spectacular feature of the distribution, however, is the marked concentration of dedications in the hinterland of the Teifi estuary. Five of the eight Welsh saints (excluding Cadog), represented in contiguous parishes in mid-Cornwall, are found within this limited area in west Wales. St. Briog is patron of Llandyfriog in the extreme south-west of Cardiganshire, and not far away on the coast are Llangrannog and Gwbert. These places are called after saints (Carannog and Gwbert respectively) who have given their names to two adjoining parishes near New Quay in Cornwall. At the present time Gwbert, near to Cardigan, is

---

[1] SS. Samson, Malo and Briog are interesting examples of this.

[2] It is of the greatest importance to distinguish on both physical and cultural grounds the seaward facing valleys and outlying peninsulas of Western Britain from other parts of the Highland Zone. The conventional division of Britain into a Highland and a Lowland Zone is a well-known and useful generalization, but a triple division into Lowland, Highland and Atlantic Britain, as suggested here, would not only be more accurate but also more helpful to scholars generally.

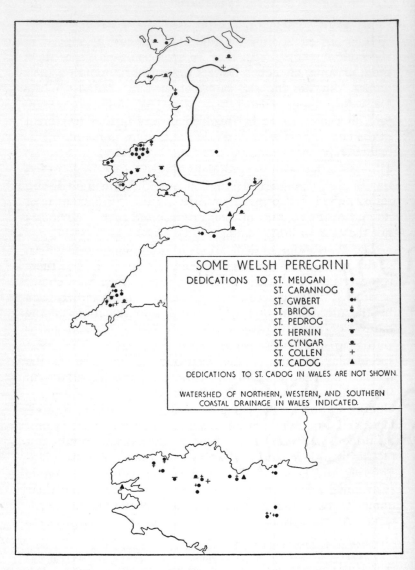

SOME WELSH PEREGRINI

DEDICATIONS TO ST. MEUGAN   ●
           ST. CARANNOG
           ST. GWBERT
           ST. BRIOG
           ST. PEDROG
           ST. HERNIN
           ST. CYNGAR
           ST. COLLEN   +
           ST. CADOG   ▲

DEDICATIONS TO ST. CADOG IN WALES ARE NOT SHOWN.

WATERSHED OF NORTHERN, WESTERN, AND SOUTHERN
COASTAL DRAINAGE IN WALES INDICATED.

Fig. 24

the name of a modern coastal settlement in the parish of
Ferwig, but on the shore there is a cave still known as
' Ogo'r Eglwys.'[1] Ferwig church is dedicated to St.
Pedrog while on the other side of the Teifi, in the parish
of Llandudoch, in Pembrokeshire, there was once an ancient
chapel dedicated to St. Carannog. A few miles southward is Llanfeugan in Cemais, the centre of the cult of St.
Meugan (Mawgan), while nearby is Llanfoygan, Pant y
Deri, Capel Meugan in Bridell parish, and a chapel and
holy well called after this saint in the parish of Llanfair Nant-
gwyn. If we bear in mind the reservations already made
concerning St. Cadog, it is still possible that the striking
recurrence of dedications to Saints Carannog, Gwbert,
Pedrog, Briog and Meugan in close proximity to each other
in the lands bordering the Teifi estuary, in mid-Cornwall,
and in northern Brittany, may contain a dim reminiscence
of historical fact—that these saints were companions in some
great missionary enterprise. Whether Cyngar, Hernin and
Collen were also involved in the same movement is less
obvious from the topographical evidence in Wales, although
they appear to be closely associated with the major group in
the Cornish and Breton evidence.[2] It is, however, interesting to note that St. Meugan, whose cult is by far the most
widespread of the group in Wales, is remembered at Trevigan
in Llanrhian not far from Llanwngar near St. David's ; while
there is a Capel Meugan near Cilmaenllwyd in western
Carmarthenshire quite close to Cilhernin, Llanboidy ; and
even in north-eastern Wales Meugan is culted at Ruthin,
Cyngar at Hope in southern Flintshire, and Collen not very
far away at Llangollen.

We can now turn to examine the persistent traditions in
Welsh hagiological literature that there were numerous
peregrini using the southern sea-route in the opposite direction,

---

[1] G. H. Doble, *St. Carantoc*, op. cit., p. 25.

[2] Doble thinks that the Cyngar dedications in Wales belong to a different
saint from the Congar remembered in Cornwall and Brittany (*Antiquity* op. cit.,
p. 34), while Crawford claims that Hernin in Llanegwad is St. Iserninus
(d. 468) and in his opinion represents one of the earliest dedications in Wales
(' Western Seaways,' op. cit., p. 190).

that is, moving from Brittany into Wales.   They are said to
have been led by St. Cadfan and to have included among
others Padarn, Tydecho, Trinio, Maelrys, Cynon, Mael,
Sulien, Eithras, Henwyn, Tannwg, Llywen, Llyfab, Tegai,
Trillo, Llechid, Dochwy, Tegwyn, Baglan, Meilyr, Fflewin,
Gredifael, Lleuddad, Sadwrn, Gwyndaf, Ilar, Cristiolus and
Rhystud.[1]   The written authority for such a list, as may be
expected, is almost entirely worthless.   Most of the above
names occur in the Peniarth, Hafod and Cardiff genealogies
of pre-sixteenth century date, as well as in the later spurious
Iolo Mss., where all sorts of embellishments are added.
Whenever a genealogy is given, these individuals are traced
back through Cadfan to his maternal grandfather, Emyr
Llydaw (Emyr of Brittany).   Since the majority of these
saints have churches dedicated to them in Wales in close
proximity to each other they have almost certainly been
made by the medieval genealogists into closely related
persons claiming descent from a traditional leader.

Before proceeding to a topographical analysis of the dedications of these saints in Wales it is worth while drawing
attention to the fact that the list contains the name of St.
Padarn, doubtless, owing to the proximity of his churches to
those of the other saints in the list (see Fig. 25).   We have
already advanced arguments for linking St. Padarn with an
earlier movement based on south-eastern Wales, and we
would consider his name to be as anomalous in this list as
St. Cadog's was in the former.   For this reason the distribution of his churches is not shown on Fig. 25.   Furthermore, scholars have questioned the whole basis of a movement, in reverse, as it were, from Brittany to Wales in the
Dark Ages.   Some, for example, have thought it as absurd
as would be a return movement originating among eighteenth century English colonists in North America to Christ-
ianize Britain,[2] yet we must remember that in the Dark Ages
there was intense activity in the western seas and folk
movements in all directions are highly probable.   The

[1] Baring Gould and Fisher, op. cit., II, pp. 1-2.
[2] G. H. Doble, *Saint Patern*, Cornish Saints Series, No. 43, 1940, p. 17.

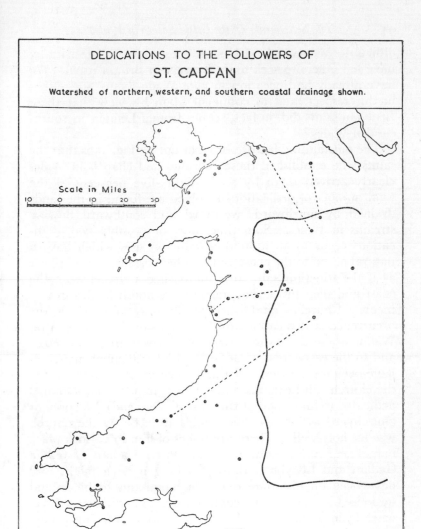

DEDICATIONS TO THE FOLLOWERS OF
ST. CADFAN

Watershed of northern, western, and southern coastal drainage shown.

Scale in Miles

Dotted lines join churches dedicated to the same
saint in a coastal and inland position

Fig. 25

difficulties associated with such an exodus from Brittany have led others to seek for a Letavia in Britain itself. We have already had occasion to note Wade-Evans' suggestion in this respect, and to comment upon his view that these Letavian saints did, in fact, set out from a Letavia in south-eastern Wales.[1]

The outstanding feature brought out by Fig. 25 is that the saints who established these churches and chapels in Wales clearly arrived there by sea. Eighty-five per cent of the total number of dedications involved are found in the lands drained by northward, westward and southward flowing streams in Wales. Sometimes one, or possibly two, dedications occur to an individual saint on sites which have a natural access to the coast, but in other cases it would appear as if the itinerant saint first established a chapel near the coast and then proceeded inland to establish further settlements. Churches established in this way account for the occurrence of dedications to Letavian saints in east-central Wales, where the natural drainage is away from the coast and to the eastwards. Cadfan's initial settlement may well have been on the west coast at Towyn in Merioneth, where the church still bears his name, while, in addition, a chapel dedicated to him stood at the north-eastern end of the present churchyard as late as 1620, and a little below the church was his holy well. There are traces of him in various place names near Abergynolwyn, such as Pistyll Cadfan, Eisteddfa Gadfan and Llwybr Cadfan.[2] Abergynolwyn might well have been on his route over the mountains to his inland station—Llangadfan, in central Montgomeryshire. Likewise, Tydecho had several cells in the western-facing valleys of Mcrioncth as, for example, at Cemais and Mallwyd, while another is located near the source of the Dyfi at Llanymawddwy, with evidence of a former chapel bearing his name in the hills nearby. Further eastwards, and beyond the watershed, the church at Garthbeibio is dedicated to him, and here we are within two miles of his kinsman's eastern

[1] See p. 55.
[2] Baring Gould and Fisher, op. cit., II. p. 6.

settlement at Llangadfan. A similar pattern emerges in other parts of Wales. Cwm church, not far from the coast in northern Flintshire, is dedicated conjointly to Saints Mael and Sulien (both followers of St. Cadfan), while far inland to the southward in the eastern flowing section of the river Dee, the parish church of Corwen is dedicated conjointly to the same saints. St. Trillo (another reputed member of the party) has a church dedicated to him at Llandrillo-yn-Rhos on the Denbighshire coast near to the modern Llandudno, while close by (and literally on the shore) are the ruins of an ancient chapel which bore his name. Here he must have landed and then moved over the Hiraethog moorlands some thirty-five miles inland to found another Llandrillo not far from Corwen, where there is a dedication to Saints Mael and Sulien. Such examples could be multiplied, and would appear to indicate a close parallel with conditions in Brittany. St. Carannog, for example, is commemorated in the parish of Carantec on the north coast of Léon, where he probably landed, while to the westward, and in a markedly inland position, there is another parish called Trégarantec, thereby following the rule laid down by M. Largillière that the saints who evangelized Brittany first lived as hermits on the shore where they landed and where there is now usually a chapel bearing their name, and afterwards moved inland to minister to the colonists there, who had recently left the mother country to found a home in Armorica.[1]

We are still left with the problem of the origin of the Cadvanian *peregrini* who settled in Wales. Did they arrive by sea from a Letavia which is Brittany, or from a district of the same name possibly in south-eastern Wales? These, of course, are questions which the map cannot claim to answer. All that can be said is that there is not a single dedication to any one of them in south-eastern Wales, so that if they derive hence they must have become saints after leaving their homeland. Three of them, however, Saints Cadfan, Sulien and Baglan are culted in Brittany and it is

[1] G. H. Doble, *St. Carantoc*, Cornish Saints Series, No. 14, 1928, pp. 24-25.

possible that St. Sulien is the patron of Luxulyan in Cornwall as well. If we reverse the view of Canon Doble regarding Welsh saints culted in Cornwall and Brittany and state that Breton saints in Wales have little or no cult in the country of their origin, then it is possible to argue that there is just sufficient evidence available for us to incline towards a Breton origin of the Cadvanian *peregrini*. It is, of course, possible that saints like Cadfan and Sulien might have visited both Wales and Brittany at different times and yet have originated outside both areas. Dedication distribution maps are, unfortunately, not track maps and can not provide us with direct evidence of where a saint began his peregrinations or of where he finished.

The part played by Irish saints in establishing settlements in Wales will next be considered. The background is provided by a survey of the cultural relationships between the two countries in prehistoric times. Ireland stands out in early times not merely as an area receiving British cultures, but also as a land possessing an active and creative life of its own, which, stimulated by seafarers and traders, invigorated not only the lands on the opposite shores of the Irish Sea but frequently influenced the mainland of Europe as well.[1] Ireland reacted similarly in the days of Celtic Christianity. In the later period, in particular, her great monasteries, such as those of Aran, Bangor, Clonard, Clonfert, Clonmacnoise and Moville became famous throughout Europe, and traces of Irish *peregrini* are found from the Plain of Lombardy in the south to Iceland in the far north. The curious feature, however, is that Irish *peregrini* have left relatively few settlements in Wales, although the contacts between the territories must have been frequent and close at this time. Indeed, the hagiological literature is suggestive of much closer contact than is indicated by surviving dedications. This statement is as true of the sixth and seventh centuries A.D., (that is, the period before the Irish monasteries embarked on their greatest missionary efforts) as it is of the succeeding period (the eighth and

[1] C. Fox, *The Personality of Britain* (4th Edit., 1943), pp. 43-44.

ninth centuries) when the fame of the Irish missionaries in Europe was at its height. Nevertheless, St. Aidan of Ferns has dedications in Wales at Llawhaden (Llanrhiadain), Nolton, Haroldston West and Solfach in Pembrokeshire, and at Llanmadog in Gower and at Capel Madog in the Elan valley in Radnorshire, if we allow that his name might occur as Madog, based on the form Mo-aid-og. Likewise, St. Colman of Dromore is probably represented at Llangolman, near Maenclochog, and again at Capel Colman in the same county, while the late Canon Fisher showed that the supposed Welsh saints Caron, Cennech, Ffinnan, Myllin, Saeran, Sannan and others were Irish bred.[1] As is to be expected, dedications to Irish saints are found for the most part in the south-western and in the north-western regions of Wales. These peninsulas would be their natural landing places and, at the same time, the areas in which they would be most likely to find other Irish settlers.

More numerous, however, than the dedications to all these saints together are the churches and chapels in Wales dedicated to St. Brigid (Bride or Ffraid) of Kildare, whose popularity can be accounted for only by the fact that she must have replaced a Celtic Fire Goddess of earlier times. Her cult appears in Ireland, Wales, Cornwall, Devon, Brittany, Cumbria and Scotland, and most likely it belonged originally to the areas which were colonized by the Irish in the fifth and sixth centuries A.D., and spread subsequently over all the Celtic lands. Fig. 26 shows how widespread are her dedications in Wales. Coastal chapels and inland churches occur in almost equal numbers. It would, however, be going beyond the purview of this book to seek a further analysis of the Ffraid dedications in Wales, in so far as they differ from most of the distributions we have been considering in that the saint herself could not conceivably have visited any of these sites in person. Furthermore, there are indications that her cult was only beginning to become popular in Wales in the eleventh century which

---

[1] J. Fisher, ' Welsh Church Dedications', *Trans. Hon. Soc. Cymmrod.* 1906-7, p. 84.

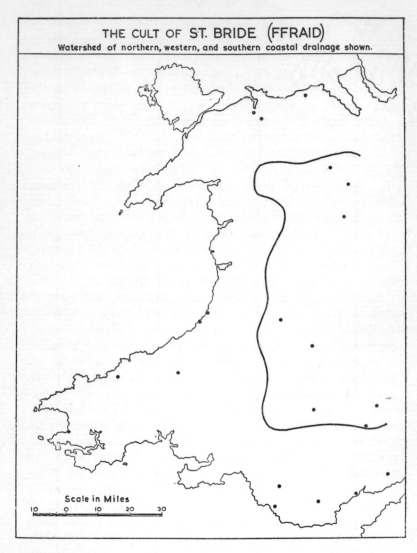

THE CULT OF ST. BRIDE (FFRAID)
Watershed of northern, western, and southern coastal drainage shown.

Scale in Miles

Fig. 26

lies considerably beyond the period we have under review.

It is fitting to close this chapter by reference to a problem that has hitherto remained untouched, namely the Celtic Saints and the Celtic languages. We have no evidence that these wandering monks were missionaries to the people at large, and judging by the size of the Irish cells associated with this period, or even those revealed by archaeological excavation in Ireland or elsewhere, there would not appear to be room inside them for congregational worship of any kind, although there was always the possibility of a Celtic recluse preaching to the people in the open air in a language they understood. However this may be, we are certain that the language of the church both in Ireland and Britain was Latin, as it was throughout Western Europe in the Middle Ages. So that the Celtic Saints in Wales and the Irish Saints who in later times visited Britain in large numbers are not likely to have spoken British or Irish together to any great extent, but Latin, the common language of the Christian Church[1].

It would appear that the missionary zeal of the Celtic Saints would be directed at winning over the local chieftain and his family and in outmanœuvring the pagan priests in attendance at Court. It was in this way that St. Columba began his mission to the Picts by visiting King Brude at his fortress at Inverness[2]. In this connection it must be remembered that a considerable element among the upper classes and in the royal households of the petty kings of the Dark Ages in Highland Britain, south of the Forth-Clyde isthmus had some knowldge of Latin—barbaric Latin though it might be. The Highland zone had experienced a re-infusion of Roman life and culture at this time coming partly as we have seen from the incursion of Gallo-Roman Christians by way of the Western Seas, who set up tombstones to *magistrati* and *cives*, and partly from refugees from the more Romanized parts of the Lowland Zone of Britain, who introduced into the West many of the

[1] Jackson, K. *Language and History in Early Britain* (Edinburgh, 1953), p. 123.
[2] Duke, J. A. *The Columban Church* (Oxford, 1936), pp. 70-75.

Latin words borrowed centuries before into their British speech, and whose Latin was still that of the British educated classes and of the church now being established in the West. Both groups were eager to show that they were the inheritors of all the greatness that was Rome and in like manner the resurgent Native Kings—the ' tyrants ' of Gildas, claimed to share in the great inheritance. Their tombstones were invariably inscribed not in British but in Latin.

The linguistic situation in Wales had been greatly complicated by the arrival of Irish settlers both in the south-west and in the north-west. In the south-west and in Brycheiniog their hold was firmly established, while at the same time we should not overlook the penetration of Irish influence along the whole of the South Wales coastal fringe by the extension of the sea routes. This is attested by archaeological evidence[1] and by the Irish form of Illtud's name preserved in Lanyltwyt or Laniltwyt before it was reduced to Llantwit[2], as well as in the traditions in the *Vita Sancti Cadoci* of that saint's influence in, and his frequent visits to, Ireland. The same source emphasizes also the fact that the most distinguished of the early Irish saints came to be Cadoc's disciples at Llancarfan. When, however, it came to the erecting of memorials to the recently arrived Irish chieftains in south-west Wales we notice that Latin was once more used alongside of Irish. Furthermore, Professor Kenneth Jackson[3] has recently shown that in Britain when an Irish king's name was to be written in Latin on his tombstone (as in the case of Voteporix king of Dyfed, who died about 550 A.D.) the British equivalent for it was used—a fact which implies the existence of British as well as Irish speakers in the community. In the north-west the Irish element does not appear to have been so strongly entrenched. The story of the Sons of Cunedda suggests that most of North Wales was occupied at the

---

[1] Fox, Aileen, *Early Christian Period* in *A Hundred Years of Welsh Archaeology*, 1846-1946. C.A.S. p. 108. note 2..

[2] see page 43.

[3] Jackson, K. op. cit. p. 169.

beginning of the fifth century by leaders, moved there as allies of the Romans, whose task it had been to drive out the Irish settlers. Such leaders recently arrived from the North would be British speakers, but most authorities now think[1] that the British Kingdoms of Southern Scotland in the Dark Ages had been founded by the Romans, under the rule of Romanized Britons as a defence against the Picts and Scots. It is likely that such Celtic chieftains and their descendants (claiming to inherit the power of the Roman Empire) had also retained some Latin for religious and epigraphical purposes. We know, for example, that Cadfan (Catamanus) a king of North Wales, who died as late as 625 A.D. had a Latin epitaph. It was found at the church of his grandson—Llangadwaladr in Anglesey.

It has frequently been argued when dedication-distributions show that the activities of certain saints are confined to specific regions and do not spread into other areas, that the differences are due to differences in language between the areas concerned. Dedication to Cadfan, Briog, Baglan, Carannog, Pedrog, Sulien and Tydecho are well represented in Wales, Cornwall and Brittany— Brittonic speaking areas, but do not appear in Ireland, Scotland and the Isle of Man—Goidelic speaking regions.

The determining factor, however, is not primarily a a linguistic one, but the fact that the Dark Ages in the west witnessed many mass migrations of peoples utilizing the sea routes as in prehistoric times, so that the dedications to the saints in question reflect their movements (or those of their followers) to and fro among their kinsmen.

An epilogue to this chapter and, indeed, to the first part of this book can do no better than to collate the major culture areas that have emerged from this study of the dedication distribution patterns of the various Celtic saints. At the same time it would be appropriate to review the

[1] See P. Hunter Blair, *Archaeologia Aeliana* xxv (1947), pp. 1ff and 19ff; and H. M. Chadwick, *Early Scotland* (Cambridge, 1949), Ch. x.

H

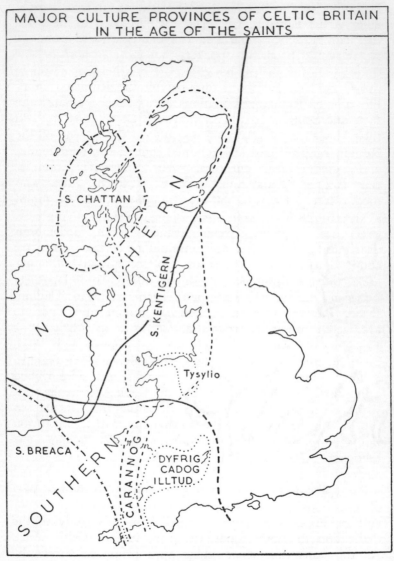

MAJOR CULTURE PROVINCES OF CELTIC BRITAIN IN THE AGE OF THE SAINTS

S. CHATTAN

NORTHERN

S. KENTIGERN

Tysylio

S. BREACA

SOUTHERN

CARANNOG

DYFRIG
CADOG
ILLTUD.

Fig. 27

Welsh evidence in the broader setting of Celtic Britain at this period. Fig. 27 provides the overall picture.

The presence of two major provinces (northern and southern) in Celtic Britain appears to have been well established. They may be said to be the territories of St. Columba and St. David respectively. North Wales and Cumbria would appear to occupy an intermediate position. Most frequently they are influenced by an overspill from the Northern province, but sometimes they feel the influence of southern cultures, as in the case of St. Cybi and the followers of St. Cadfan. At other times, North Wales and Cumbria appear to be untouched by either northern or southern influences as happened in the case of St. Columba and St. David respectively.

Within the major provinces a number of sub-provinces are clearly marked. Some of these do not touch Wales, as, for example, the *patria* of St. Chattan in Antrim and western Scotland, or that of St. Breaca and her followers in south-western Ireland and the Land's End district of Cornwall.

In Wales itself the North and South are fundamentally different in their cultural associations. The North was certainly drawn within the Kentigern province, and what may be termed the Gwynedd and the Powys sub-regions are persistently marked—sometimes, within the same cult, as with Cyndeyrn or Beuno, but, at other times, an individual saint like Tysilio characterizes one only of the sub-regions.

In South Wales we find the Dyfrig-Cadog-Illtud sub-province in the south-east which was treated in Chapter II and which extends along the Somerset-Devon coast into Mid-Cornwall and thence into Brittany. To the westward in South Wales is the Carannog sub-province which includes dedications to so many '*peregrini.*' It reaches from south-western Cardiganshire, through Pembrokeshire and western Carmarthenshire into Mid-Cornwall and thence into Brittany. The country between the Dyfrig-Cadog-Illtud sub-province and that of Carannog in South Wales may be said to be the particular *patria* of the Children of Brychan.

PART II

CHAPTER VI

THE DISTRIBUTION OF CELTIC CHURCHES—A STUDY OF POSITION

T HE second part of this book deals with historical geography in the strict sense of the term. We shall be concerned in the first instance with the relationship between the overall pattern formed by the distribution of Celtic churches and the broad outlines of the physical geography of Wales and the Border country. We can then proceed to an examination of the more detailed problems associated with the precise siting of the churches in a subsequent chapter.

The overall distribution of ancient churches and chapels dedicated to Celtic saints either now existing, or known to have existed in the past, is shown on Fig. 28. The picture is by no means a complete one for when all the known information has been collected we are clearly dealing with what might be termed a residual pattern. We have now no means of knowing how many monastic cells were originally established by the Celtic saints in what is today Wales and the territory lying beyond its eastern frontiers. Many of them must have vanished, leaving no vestige of their existence either in written records or in the present landscape.[1] Furthermore, as was made clear in the introductory

---

[1] The extent of what has vanished is revealed in a startling manner when we chance upon an early topographical record, as, for example, that provided by George Owen of Henllys for his native Cemais in north-eastern Pembrokeshire in Elizabethan times. He tells us of ' Capellas olim peregrinationis causa erectus quorum nunc pars maxima dilabuntur' :

Capel Carannog	} St. Dogmaels.	Capel Cavey	} Mynachllog
Capel Degwel	}	Capel St. Silin	} Ddu.
Capel St. Fraid	}	Capel Llanmerchan,	Llanychllwy-
Capel Gwenfron	}		ddog
Capel Gwenddydd,	} Nevern	Capel Dewi	}
Capel Reall	}	Capel Curig	} Newport
Capel Padric	}	Capel Mewgan, Bridell.	
Capel Brynach, Morvil.		Capel Wrw, Eglwys Wrw.	
		Capel Brynach, ' Henry's Moat.'	

George Owen, *The Description of Pembrokeshire*, Cymmrod. Series Part 2, p. 509.

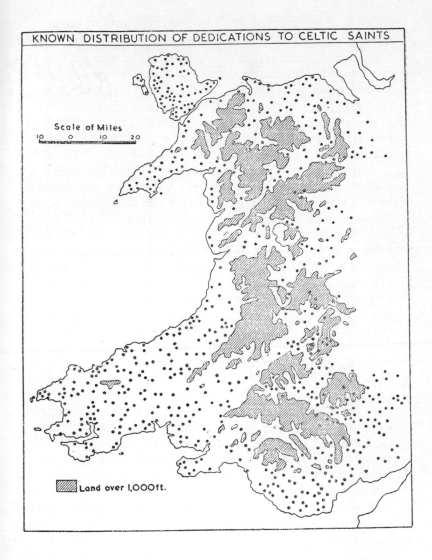

Fig. 28

chapter many originally Celtic churches have long since had their dedications changed to suit Norman and later fashions. Unfortunately, we are not able to be certain in several suspected cases that a change was actually made. All that we are certain of is that the changes that have been made must influence very considerably the distribution pattern shown on Fig. 28. One of the chief features brought out by the map is the relative sparsity of Celtic dedications in the thoroughly Normanized areas. Flintshire provides a striking example. Here we have a low-lying area backed by the Clwydian range which was easily dominated by the Norman lordship of Chester. Almost two-thirds of the parish churches in this county are now dedicated to Biblical saints and to members of the Holy Family, while dedications to St. Mary are extremely popular. A similar replacement of dedications to Celtic saints must have taken place throughout the Border country, perhaps, as early as the Saxon conquest. It is most important to realize that the influence of the Celtic church must have reached far into what is now south-western England previous to the expansion and consolidation of Wessex. Dr. O. G. S. Crawford[1] has pointed out that during the Roman occupation the route from South Wales to the Continent would have been from Abone at the mouth of the Bristol Avon along the Roman road by way of Bath, Marlborough and Silchester to London, thence to Canterbury and Richborough. It would appear that this route was still being used in the early Dark Ages by travellers from the West as witnessed by the extraordinary Ogham inscribed stone found in a well in the Roman town of Silchester.[2] Celtic saints, doubtless, used the same route. We know of St. Cain (Keyne) and St. Maeldubh who founded religious communities at Keynsham on the Avon, between Bristol and Bath, and at Malmesbury respectively, but if the legends of their foundation contain any substratum of historical fact, as they almost certainly do, then they indicate very clearly the onetime more extensive

[1] O. G. S. Crawford, ' Western Seaways,' op. cit., p. 188.
[2] See *Archaeologia* LIV, pp. 223, 241.

patria of the Celtic saints. In this context it is well to remember that relief has played an important part in retarding and modifying both the Saxon and the Norman penetration of the Celtic lands. The mountainous terrain and deep sheltered valleys of south-western Herefordshire present a complete contrast to the neighbouring Hereford plain. The plain lost its Celtic speech and presumably its Celtic dedications at an early date, while Celtic speech survived in south-western Herefordshire for at least two hundred years after the Act of Union with England (1536), and churches dedicated to famous Celtic saints are still found in the area.

Having drawn attention to the way in which the original distribution of Celtic dedications must have been considerably modified both on the eastern Border and along the southern sea-plain, we can now return to consider further features of the general distribution pattern. In brief, it may be said that Celtic dedications occur in all districts except the higher mountain lands and the marshes (see Fig. 28). Low-lying land and the lower valley-slopes were clearly favoured. A recent study of the distribution of Celtic keills in the Isle of Man reveals precisely similar features.[1] It is worthwhile, therefore, making a more detailed analysis of the altitudes at which the Celtic Christian churches in Wales are found. Fig. 29 attempts to represent graphically for each county the precise altitude above sea-level of the individual churches shown on Fig. 28. The altitude in each case has been read off the six inches to a mile Ordnance Survey sheets. The counties are arranged in their order of altitude from Caernarvonshire (which has the highest altitude) to nearby Anglesey which has the lowest. Each county column represents the *lowest* third of the county's altitudinal range. Thus, for example, in Caernarvonshire where the highest point is 3560 feet, the lowest third of its altitudinal range will be within wide limits, ranging from sea-level to 1187 feet, while in Anglesey where the highest elevation is approximately 720 feet the lowest

[1] C. J. S. Marstrander, *Journ. of the Manx Museum*, IV, 1938.

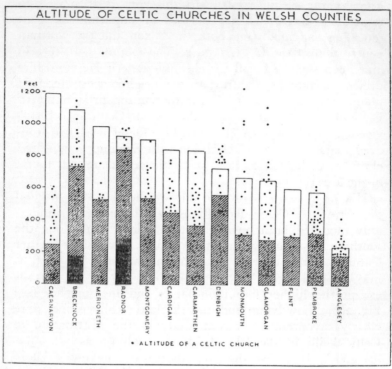

Fig. 29

For details of the height of the columns and shading see this page.

third of the range will be between the relatively narrow limits from sea-level to 240 feet. Two counties, Brecknock and Radnor have no coastline and their lowest altitudes are 180 feet and 300 feet respectively. The lowest third of the altitudinal range in such cases has been calculated in a similar manner but obviously from these base-lines and not from sea-level. Against each column so prepared has been plotted (using the same vertical scale) the altitude of all the Celtic churches in the respective counties. A line has been drawn separating the upper third of their number in each county from the lower two-thirds, the altitudinal range of the latter being shaded in each case (see Fig. 29).

An analysis of these data for the whole of Wales is revealing. In each county two-thirds of the total number of ancient Celtic churches lie within the lowest third of the county's altitudinal range, while in Flint, Carmarthen, Caernarvon, Cardigan, and Montgomery *all* the Celtic churches are in the lowest third of their respective county's altitudinal range (Fig. 29). It should be noted, too, that in counties such as Caernarvon and Anglesey where the lowest third of the altitudinal range lies within wide and narrow limits respectively, two-thirds of the Celtic churches lie *in both cases* below 250 feet (Fig. 29). Even in counties such as Brecknock and Radnor where the altitude above sea-level of the majority of Celtic churches is greater than elsewhere in Wales, two thirds of their number in each case fall easily within the lowest third of the actual altitudinal range of the territories concerned.

The county diagrams as a whole confirm the general impression obtained from Fig. 28 and show very clearly how the founders of Celtic churches in Wales chose, on the whole, the lower lands in each of the counties irrespective of absolute altitude. Before proceeding to a further discussion of this matter, we must turn aside to examine another aspect of the distribution pattern shown on Fig. 28.

The dense grouping of Celtic churches in the northwestern and south-western peninsulas respectively is clearly apparent. These concentrations are by no means due entirely to the general lowlying character of the regions concerned. In attempting to account for them we must recollect the extensive use made by the Celtic saints of the western sea-routes. The areas showing the densest groupings are Anglesey, Arfon and Llŷn in the north, while in the south-west the whole of Pembrokeshire together with south-western Cardiganshire and the western half of Carmarthenshire are involved. These western peninsulas of Wales are natural landing stages projecting into the western seas. As such, they possess a rich record of cultures that habitually used the thalassic routes. The distribution of Celtic churches in these parts suggests that their founders were real settlers and not travellers only. If the latter had been the case the Celtic churches would have been more clearly distributed athwart the peninsulas in the manner of several prehistoric distributions indicating a well-marked transpeninsular route. On the contrary, settlement in close proximity to the sea or to tidal water is in evidence and may be considered as another factor of much significance in analysing the general location of Celtic churches in Wales, as, indeed, it would appear to be in all Celtic lands.[1] In the north-western and south-western peninsulas proximity to the sea or to tidal water is possible over extensive areas— there is no part of the entire county of Pembroke, for example, which is more than eight miles from tidal water. The extent of similar areas along the northern, south-eastern and western coasts of Wales, is, for obvious geographical reasons more restricted. Nevertheless, even in areas where the mountains come close to the coast, as in Merioneth, we find that all the churches of Ardudwy (with the exception of Trawsfynydd) are actually within sight of the sea. This is particularly true of such churches as Maentwrog, Ffestiniog and Llandecwyn which stood originally much nearer to the sea than they do today, at a time when the Traeth Bach extended much further inland, and before the ingenuity of Mr. Madocks had 'reclaimed' these estuarine flats in the early nineteenth century.[2]

We must now attempt to relate the distribution of the Celtic churches to that of the native settlement pattern in Wales. The first thing that we are certain of is that immediately prior to the Roman occupation the native peoples lived on the uplands, in or near to their hill-forts. These are found not in the mountain country proper, but on the lower slopes and saddles of the hill-country, usually between altitudes of 400 and 1000 feet. Fig. 30 shows the relative altitudes of the Iron Age hill-forts and the Celtic

---

[1] G. H. Doble, *Four Saints of the Fal*, Cornish Saints Series, No. 20, 1929, p. 2.

[2] R. Richards, ' Ardudwy and its Ancient Churches', *Harlech Studies* (Cardiff 1938), p. 174.

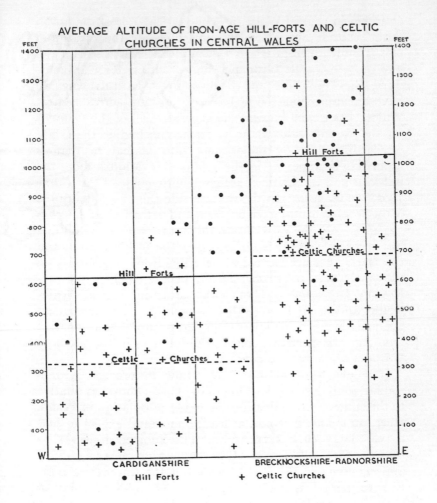

AVERAGE ALTITUDE OF IRON-AGE HILL-FORTS AND CELTIC CHURCHES IN CENTRAL WALES

CARDIGANSHIRE BRECKNOCKSHIRE-RADNORSHIRE

● Hill Forts   + Celtic Churches

Fig. 30

churches in central Wales.[1]   The vertical axis of the graph shows altitude above sea-level in feet while the horizontal axis is built up from selected grid-lines (' eastings ') on the one inch to a mile Ordnance Survey sheets for Cardiganshire, Brecknockshire and Radnorshire.   In this way we have an approximate west to east gradation across central Wales.   As is well known, the general relief of the counties on the eastern side of the watershed is higher than that of Cardiganshire on the western side—a feature that is immediately apparent in the relative elevation of both the hill-forts and the Celtic churches on either side of the watershed.   (Fig. 30).   On the western side the average altitude of the Iron Age hill-forts is 621 feet, and of the Celtic churches 328 feet.   On the eastern side the figures are 1030 and 692 feet respectively.   It is obvious that the Celtic churches of the Dark Ages are located at very much lower altitudes on the whole than those whereon the people dwelt in the pre-Roman Iron Age.   The Celtic saints in central Wales would appear to have settled in country that was on an average some 300 feet lower than that occupied in the native Iron Age, irrespective of marked differences in the absolute altitudes of the regions concerned.

It would be ideal if we were now to proceed with a similar analysis of the location of the Celtic churches relative to the contemporary distribution of the population in Wales. Here, on *a priori* grounds, at least, one would expect to find a reasonably close correlation.   The subject, however, is fraught with difficulties.   Our knowledge of the habitat and economy of the Welsh people in the immediate post-Roman period is by no means as extensive as that of immediate pre-Roman times.   Nash-Williams and Savory[2] have, however, begun to elucidate the problem.   They have pointed out that while many, if not most, of the native hill-

[1] The data regarding the hill-forts are based on V. E. Nash-Williams, *Arch. Camb.*, LXXXVIII, Pt. 2, 1933, pp. 311-346;   revised for Brecknockshire and Radnorshire *Bull. Board of Celtic Studies*, xiv, 1950, pp. 69-75 and xv, 1952, pp. 73-80 respectively.
[2] V. E. Nash-Williams and H. N. Savory, ' The Distribution of Hill-Forts', *Bull. Board of Celtic Studies*, 1949, pp. 152-3.

forts were occupied during the Roman period, few new ones were built. Roman rulers would regard with disfavour the erection of what were in fact fortified villages and temporary refuges for a district. On the contrary, the small homestead type of camp (usually less than about two acres in extent) and functioning as a defended farmstead, or the headquarters of an estate, continued to be occupied, or even built, during the Roman period. Thus, it is argued that earthworks represented by small concentric enclosures and rectangular defended homesteads on low plateaux and hillslopes were the representative native settlements of the late Roman period and the Dark Ages. More recently, however, Savory is inclined to the view that these structures are Iron Age in origin and differ from the larger hill-forts in that they continued to be occupied throughout the Roman period on into the Dark Ages.[1] An attempt has been made on Fig. 31 to show the distribution of these smaller earth-

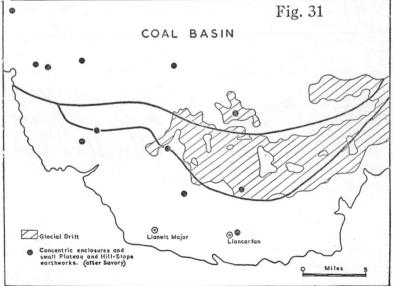

Fig. 31

COAL BASIN

Glacial Drift

Llanwit Major

Llancarfan

Concentric enclosures and small Plateau and Hill-Slope earthworks. (after Savory)

Miles

The heavy lines represent the margins of the 400 ft. platform. To the south are the remnants of the 200 ft. platform.

[1] H. N. Savory, 'The Hill-Forts of Brecknockshire', *Bull. Board of Celtic Studies*, XIV, Pt. I, 1950, p. 70.

works in Glamorgan.   We find them largely on the southern margins of the coal-basin, or on the remaining fragments of the 200 foot erosion platform of the ' Vale of Glamorgan.' It would appear, therefore, that during the Dark Ages the native peoples were, in the main, occupying the lower country of the ' Vale ' and its margins, whereon the Romans had placed their villas and other settlements.   If the Glamorgan evidence can be taken as representative of the whole of Wales then we can say that in the Dark Ages the major part of the Welsh population was concentrated on the lower fringes of the hill-land.   This may be just another way of saying that one of the chief changes in the distribution of population in Britain, following upon the Roman occupation, was the gradual valley-ward movement of the people.   In the lowlands of eastern England the movement was from the chalk and gravel lands out on to the clays, but in the uplands of the west it was from the more open heights to the more sheltered valley-benches and lower plateau surfaces.[1] When we examine the sites of the surviving Celtic churches in relation to these homesteads of the Dark Ages in any specific locality we find that they tend to occupy sites at still lower elevations, frequently on, or very near to, the valley floors.   Sir Cyril and Lady Fox have instanced a striking example of this in Radnorshire.   In Swydd Buddugre in Maelienydd are found a number of pre-Norman platform farmsteads similar to those on Gelligaer Common, Glamorgan (see note below).   They are on the brink of the hills while the important Celtic churches of the district Llanbister, Llanwynno and Llanbadarn Fynydd are situated either on, or very close to, the valley floor of the Ithon and certainly well below the native farmsteads of that period. Observers are forced to the conclusion that the evangelization of this region in the Dark Ages was apparently the work of men who had no liking for the uplands.[2]

[1] Sir Cyril and Lady Fox have surveyed and described a group of early (Dark Ages) Welsh homesteads on the lower plateau fringes of Glamorgan. See *Arch. Camb*. XCIV pt. 2, 1939, pp. 163-199.

[2] Cyril and Aileen Fox, *Arch. Camb*. C, Pt. I, 1948, pp. 104-6.

We cannot dismiss this study of the relationship between the Celtic saints and the contemporary centres of population in Wales without also considering some of the cultural factors involved. We have already seen that we have little evidence that these wandering monks were missionaries to the people at large, or that their churches were established for congregational worship. It would appear that among their settlements were a number of large monastic establishments such as Nantcarban, Llanilltud Fawr and Penmon, founded possibly as missionary stations and continued as schools of learning. From these centres monks would proceed on their missionary work which would involve frequently a visit of evangelization to the court of the local chieftain. If the mission were successful, the Chieftain would, doubtless, allow the erection of a small church on his land, or, perhaps, even within his own fortified enclosure. All this work has to be clearly offset from the deep desire of these monks, sooner or later, ' to seek the desert.' This urge was a deep-rooted feature of the Celtic Church derived ultimately from the early Christian hermits of the Egyptian desert. In the Celtic Lands ' seeking the desert' meant going away from the centres of population generally and seeking desolate places, on mountain tops, on stormy headlands, on islands off the shore, as well as in the deep and dark recesses of the forested valleys. In such places the saint would set up his little church, or cell, that would subsequently be named after him, even when he had left it to his followers and moved on to yet more desolate spots. Such clearings on alluvial-fans or on river-terraces in valley bottoms, each with its tiny church and a few wattle and daub buildings, may well have appeared from above as an island, or ' ynys,' in a tree-filled loch. Around such clearings in later times farmsteads and homes might gather. The distinction between the numerous hermitages of individual saints and the larger monastic establishments, which are referred to by later writers as the ' mother churches ' of a neighbourhood, helps us to interpret much of the material shown on Figs. 28, 29 and 30.

With reference to the geographical position of the ' mother churches ' themselves there are strong *a priori* grounds for thinking that they were located nearer to the areas of contemporary settlement. Their distribution (Fig. 32) merely shows them to be peripheral to the central highland area in a manner similar to that of the distribution of Celtic churches generally. In Anglesey, Ralegh Radford[1] has shown that the large monasteries of Caergybi (Holyhead) and Penmon are near to large villages which were inhabited in the immediate post-Roman centuries, and that a concentration of similar settlement-remains occurs near Llangaffo, which was the site of another large Celtic monastery near the centre of the island. If we recall the Glamorgan evidence we note that it tends to confirm that of Anglesey. Llancarfan (Nantcarban) and Llanilltud Fawr must have been very important centres and, doubtless, settlements of some size. At the same time as these monasteries flourished there is reason to think that peoples from the ' hills ' were also moving into the ' vale.' So it would appear that the larger monastic establishments of the Celtic saints were not located in such ' desert ' places (*eremum*) as those so eagerly sought after by the anchorites.

In summary, therefore, it can be said that the majority of settlements established by the saints in Wales are in the lowlying parts of the country, on the lower valley-slopes and on the valley-floors, and especially in close proximity to the sea and to tidal waters. While such a distribution is hardly correlated with the known contemporary distribution of population, it represents, nevertheless, a delicately adjusted balance between a wide range of cultural and physical factors.

[1] Roy. Comm. Anc. Mont. (Wales) *Anglesey*, 1937. General Survey. pp. xci-xcii.

THE KNOWN 'MOTHER CHURCHES' ('CLAS' CHURCHES)
OF WALES

Scale in Miles
10   0   10   20

Caer Gybi
Ynys Seiriol
Penmon
Abergele
Bangor
Llanelwy
Llanynys
Clynnog
Bangor
Iscoed
Aberdaron
Llanrhaeadr
Meifod
Towyn
Llandinam
Llanbadarn
Fawr
Llangurig
St. Harmons
Llanddewibrefi
Glascwm
Moccas
Glasbury
Tyddewi
Llandeilo
Fawr
Dewchurch
Llanarthne
Garway
Welsh
Bicknor
Penally
Llangyfelach
Caerwent
Llandeilo
Ferwallt
Llandough
Llanilltud   Llancarfan
Fawr

Land over
1,000 ft.

(after Rees, with modifications)

Fig. 32

CHAPTER VII

THE LOCATION OF CELTIC CHURCHES
A STUDY OF SITE

THE previous chapter dealt with the general distribution of the Celtic settlements in Wales, leaving for further consideration the more detailed question of the precise siting of the individual churches. In some cases, it would appear that the saints were offered existing sites for their new churches as seems to have happened when Maelgwn Gwynedd, the notorious sixth century prince of the House of Cunedda, is said to have given St. Cybi the late Roman fort on Holy Island, which has since been known as Caer Gybi (Holyhead). While there are no actual remains of any early ecclesiastical settlement within the perimeter of the fort, we may assume that the present fourteenth century church occupies the site of St. Cybi's original cell (see Fig. 33). In this connection we are reminded of similar grants of fortified dwellings made to St. Patrick and to other Celtic saints by newly converted chieftains, and, indeed, if we are to accept literally the statements in the ' Lives ' of the Irish saints it would appear that the chieftain on conversion handed over his ' dun,' or fortified homestead, to the church, and a community of monks was installed therein engaged upon missionary work within the chieftain's territory. There is good archaeological evidence indicating that the religious community normally occupied a portion of the donated ' dun ' while the chieftain retained the rest.[1] Likewise, a recent study of the geographical distribution of the Keills in the Isle of Man has shown that there appears to be one on every treen, or ancient family estate, which suggests a similar origin.[2]

[1] P. Power, ' The Bounds and Extents of Irish Parishes', *Feilscribhinn Torna* (Cork University Press : 1947), p. 219.
[2] C. J. S. Marstrander, ' The Distribution of Keills in the Isle of Man', *Journ. of the Manx Museum*, Vol. IV, 1938, p. 41.

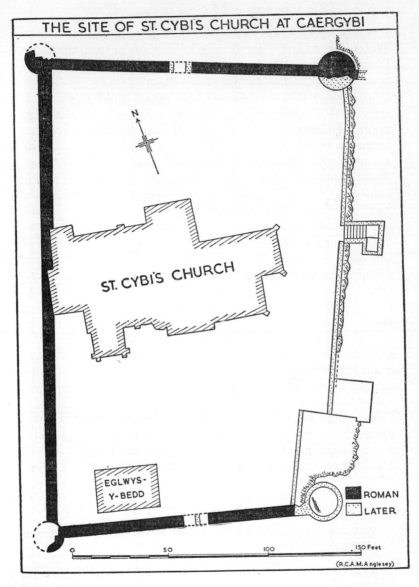

THE SITE OF ST. CYBI'S CHURCH AT CAERGYBI

N

ST. CYBI'S CHURCH

EGLWYS-
Y-BEDD

ROMAN
LATER

0   50   100   150 Feet

(R.C.A.M. Anglesey)

Fig. 33

It is, however, hardly likely that such a pattern occurred in Wales in the Dark Ages, if only in view of the semi-nomadic life practised by the free tribesmen, and the fact that there is not a single well-authenticated instance of a Celtic church established within the defences of a native hill-fort or Dark Age fortified homestead.[1]   Nevertheless, we must not look upon the Caergybi example as entirely exceptional, for other instances are known of a Celtic saint establishing his cell on a derelict Roman site as at Caerhun, Caer-went and Caer-lleon.   In these instances, however, we have no traditional evidence, as at Caergybi, that the sites were donated by a local chieftain.   The saints in question may have merely appropriated a disused site.[2]   In brief, the evidence from Wales is unquestionably weighted in favour of the view that the sites selected by the Celtic saints for their oratories and monasteries in the Dark Ages were almost invariably new ones.   There were naturally exceptions, as we have seen, but even if the exceptions were very much more numerous than the surviving evidence allows us to compute, it would not alter the central theme of this chapter, for the main consideration of the geographer is to relate the sites of these churches (whether they were established in the first instance on virgin ground or not) to the local aspects of relief, slope, soil, drainage and water supply.

Every site has been examined at some time or other both cartographically and in the field.   While it is manifestly impossible to present all the evidence in a brief survey of this kind, it is reasonable in the interests of continuity that

[1] Llanwino church in western Carmarthenshire is said to be an example, see Roy. Commission on Ancient Mont. (Wales.) *Carmarthenshire*, Vol. 5. 1917.   No. 589.

[2] We cannot rule out the possibility that the saints sometimes seized upon sites of traditional sanctity from remote prehistoric times, such as sacred wells or burial places.   Numerous examples can be cited from Brittany.   It has been suggested (H. J. Fleure and H. J. E. Peake, *Merchant Ventures in Bronze*, (*Corridors of Time*), Vol. VII, 1931, pp. 38-40), that the church of Ysbyty Cynfyn in north Cardiganshire is an example in Wales.   In spite of the present name the church is said to be a typical Celtic cell, becoming an ' Ysbyty ' in the Middle Ages.   It is placed within what appears to be the remains of a former megalithic circle ; but evidence, as in the case of so many other examples cited in Wales, leaves the matter open to considerable doubt.

examples should be selected for study from those parts of the Principality where Celtic dedications are most numerous. It will be recalled that the areas concerned are the coastal districts and valley-lands of Wales ; dependent on the one hand on the extensive use made of the sea-routes by the Saints in their travels, and on the other, by the way in which they anticipated the valley-ward movement of population in the western lands. In making this selection we must not assume that the upland areas of Wales are devoid of Celtic churches, or that their sites are unworthy of attention. So that a complete picture may be presented a short section on upland sites will follow the major discussion.

Figs. 34-36 show three representative examples of coastal sites. About a mile east of the Sarn peninsula in Llŷn, Caernarvonshire, are two tiny islands, now known as St. Tudwal's Island East and St. Tudwal's Island West. Both islands are rugged and reach over 100 feet and are built of igneous rock similar to that found on the mainland. On the eastern island (the larger of the two) there was formerly a small chapel dedicated to St. Tudwal, which is mentioned in the Taxatio of 1291, as ' Eccl'ia Prioris de Enys Tudwal.' By Leland's time it had been abandoned[1] and was subsequently converted into a barn. The chapel itself was situated in a sheltered position on the eastern side of the island above a landing place on the shore. A spring occurs a short distance away. Island sites such as this were greatly favoured by the saints and several instances occur around the Welsh coast—a picturesque example being that of St. Tysilio's church on an island in the Menai Straits. The fame of Bardsey Island as the Afallon of Saints is a frequently recurring theme in the hagiological literature.

The now disused church of Llandannwg on the Merioneth coast stands on a sandy foreshore close to the limit of High Water at the present time. It is certain, however, that when this cell was first established it lay further inland.[2] In the

---

[1] Leland, *Itin*, V, folio 50.
[2] J. A. Steers, *The Coastline of England and Wales* (1946), p. 140, and R. Richards and R. G. Lloyd, ' The Old Church of Llandanwg', *Arch. Cam^h*. Vol. XC, Pt. i, 1935, p. 70.

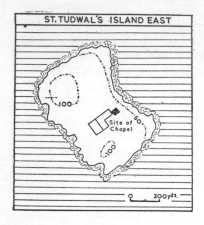

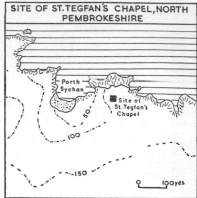

Fig. 34

Fig. 35

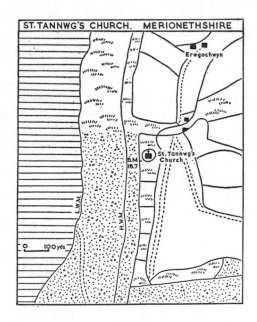

Fig. 36

course of time the sea has encroached upon the land and, in particular, the strong sea-winds have heaped up the sand-dunes against the church. It would have been completely overcome by the encroaching sand if measures had not been taken to protect it. We have no record, of course, of the actual physical condition of this part of the coast at the time when St. Tannwg established his original cell, but judging by several well-known examples elsewhere in Wales, of which St. Illtud's church at Pen-bre in south-eastern Carmarthenshire may be cited, the Celtic saints (approaching presumably from the sea) frequently chose what may be described as ' fall-line ' sites between the nearby mountain country and the lowlying sea-plain. Llandannwg might have been so situated in the Age of the Saints.

St. Tegfan's chapel is situated on the exposed cliffs of the Pen-caer peninsula in the parish of Llanwnda in north Pembrokeshire about two miles north-west of the parish church. The cliffs are of diabase—a hard, erosion-resisting rock, and they fall precipitously into the open sea. It would appear in this case as if the saint who established this cell landed in the Porthsychan cove below, and having made a steep ascent of the cliff, established a little oratory to commemorate his safe landing. Similar sites abound : there is Llanbadrig (St. Patrick's chapel) on the rocky coast of north Anglesey, while Llanaber on the exposed Merioneth coast, just north of Barmouth, is another striking example. The latter houses two of the earliest Christian inscribed stones known in Wales ; both of which were found within three-quarters of a mile of the church.[1]

The churches whose sites are shown on Figs. 34-36 clearly belong as a class to the ' hermit cell ' type, although Llandannwg was used at one time as a parish church. They do not belong to the larger monastic type of settlement also found in the Age of the Saints. It should be observed, however, that a very large proportion of the latter class are likewise found in coastal areas and in some

[1] V. E. Nash-Williams, *The Early Christian Monuments of Wales* (Cardiff, 1950), Nos. 271 and 272.

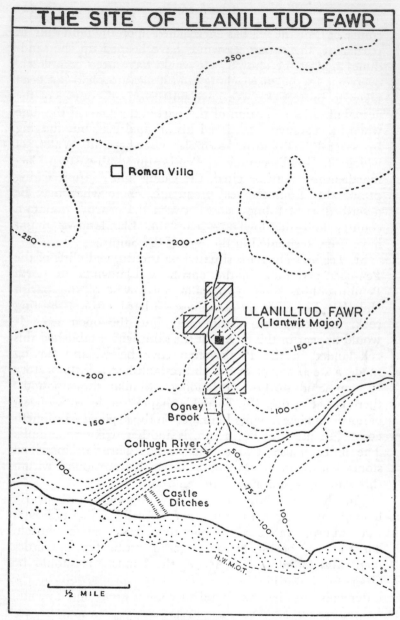

Fig. 37

instances a considerable settlement has gathered around the church in the course of time. The presumed site of St. Illtud's famous monastery at Llanilltud Fawr may be taken as an example. Fig. 37 shows that the church at Llanilltud is situated in the valley of the small Ogney stream which is a tributary of the Colhugh river. The drainage flows off the remnants of the 200 foot plateau of south Glamorgan, and the lower section of the Colhugh river (after receiving the Ogney brook) reaches the sea in a deeply incised valley. It is clear that extensive rejuvenation has taken place as a result of the uplift of these coastal margins in Tertiary times, and so there is a marked difference between the broader, open, more mature upper portions of the Ogney brook, and the lower, deeply incised portion of the Colhugh. The map shows some of the sites selected in this area by inhabitants who preceded the Celtic saints. Iron Age peoples selected the mouth of the valley and drew across the neck of a natural promontory the ramparts now known as the Castle Ditches, while inland, on the plateau surface, above the source of the Ogney the Romans established one of the largest villas in Wales. St. Illtud, however, (if his monastery lay beneath the present church and churchyard) had other ideas. He placed his monastery along the banks of the Ogney, in a broad open basin well above those portions of the topography most affected by rejuvenation. This, undoubtedly, gave him some of the best agricultural land in the area as well as all the benefits to be derived from the shelter which the basin-like form of the Ogney valley would provide. His site, however, had one other advantage ; it had direct access to, but was actually invisible from, the sea. The sharp bend at the confluence of the streams and the deeply incised character of the Colhugh hid the settlement from the many pirates who infested the western seas between the fifth and tenth centuries A.D. Some such sites were, however, discovered by pirates because the written records of this period are full of references to repeated assaults by them on coastal monasteries in Wales. An examination of the siting of many Celtic churches along the Welsh coast, nevertheless, brings out very clearly the way in which valleys that are deeply incised near their mouths and have a marked change of direction a short distance inland, have been chosen by the Celtic saints for the location of their cells.   These are placed beyond a bend in the main valley or, as at Llanilltud, on a tributary stream so as to obtain the maximum coverage from the relief and, possibly, shelter from strong sea-winds at the same time. Llancarfan and Llanedern in southern Glamorgan, and the Patron Saint's own ' podum ' in Glyn Rhosyn (St. David's) are other excellent examples.

The study of Llanilltud Fawr has already introduced us to an examination of valley-sites and so to the second major consideration of this chapter.   If we envisage the relief of Wales as a whole, we find it to consist of a highland mass reaching from Snowdonia through the Berwyn mountains, Cader Idris, Pumlumon and the Brecon Beacons on to the uplands of the southern coal basin.   The mountain core is fronted, particularly on its southern, western and north-western sides by a fringe of coastal plateaux of varying but lower altitude, formed by prolonged erosion.   The actual surfaces of these plateaux are undergoing active erosion by the numerous rivers forming part of the radial drainage of the Principality, so that the surfaces recognizable today are fractionated.   In spite of this, geomorphologists have been able to recognize several surfaces.   Dr. Greenly has demonstrated the existence of the Menai platform and other surfaces in Anglesey,[1] while Professor Miller has written on the 250 foot and the 500 foot platforms of Herefordshire and Monmouthshire,[2] and the 600 foot platform of Pembrokeshire and Carmarthenshire,[3] and, more recently, Dr. E. H. Brown has worked on the plateau surfaces of

---

[1] E. Greenly, *The Geology of Anglesey*.   2 Vols.   H.M.S.O.   1919.

[2] A. A. Miller, ' The Entrenched Meanders of the Herefordshire Wye', *Geog. Journ.* LXXXV, Pt. I, 1935, p. 180 ff.

[3] A. A. Miller, ' The 600 ft. Platform in Pembrokeshire and Carmarthen-shire', *Geog. Journ.* XC, 1937, Pt. 2, p. 150 ff.

north Cardiganshire.[1] We can now proceed to the consideration of the siting of Celtic churches within sample areas in this type of country : the first area is on the borders of Pembrokeshire and Carmarthenshire, the second in the Isle of Anglesey, and the third in the middle Ystwyth valley, while the fourth (selected so as to include examples in the deep and narrow valleys of the mountain country proper) —includes portions of the Tanad, Cain and Efyrnwy valleys of southern Denbighshire. For three of the four areas we are fortunate in possessing a detailed knowledge of the drift as well as of the solid geology.

Professor Miller has shown that most of the country represented on Fig. 38 forms an outlier of the 600 foot plateau of north Carmarthenshire and Pembrokeshire.

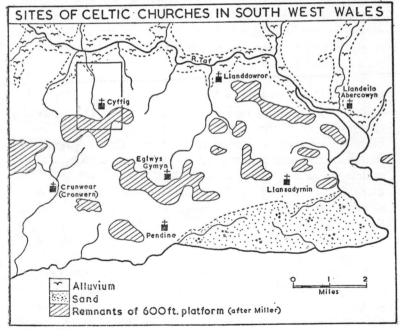

Fig. 38

[1] E. H. Brown, ' Erosion Surfaces in North Cardiganshire', *Trans. and Papers Inst. of British Geographers*, No. 16, 1950, pp. 51-56.

This plateau is developed mainly on the outcrop of the Old Red Sandstone marls, but it also extends northwards onto the Lower Palaeozoic rocks, and southwards so as to include outcrops of Carboniferous Limestone and Millstone Grit. Its surface is much broken up owing to the rapid erosion of streams draining to the Tywi, the Taf or to the coast.[1] It is clear that the valleys of these streams have been rejuvenated in recent geological times, the rejuvenation working headwards so that while the upper reaches of the valleys show all the indications of maturity, their lower portions, as they enter the sea or join a main valley, appear more gorge-like and youthful.[2]   With the exception of the wide stretches of alluvium covering the larger valley-floors, and the blown sand and shingle of the beaches, this countryside is not heavily covered by superficial deposits.   A smear of boulder clay lies across the south-western quadrant of the region, but on the valley sides the boulder clay is absent, while at the same time there would appear to be no appreciable development of river terraces.

Seven churches in all, with evidence of their being established by Celtic saints, are found within the area.   The first thing to notice about their location is that all of them avoid the remnants of the plateau surface as well as the damp alluvial stretches of the valley floors.   Five of them are found in the upper, more open, more mature sectors of their valleys, as was the case at Llanilltud Fawr ;   while two of them, Llanddowror and Llandeilo Abercowyn are at the exits of their valleys and carefully sited above the broad alluvial floor of the Taf.   It is not the lowland sites, however, that are the most significant in the area as a whole (or, for that matter, in Wales as a whole) but, on the contrary, those which utilize the broad, upper, open slopes of the valleys. Fig. 39 shows this in detail for one of the sites.   To the southwards a portion of the 600 foot plateau is clearly seen, then follows the broad sweep of the contours down to the 400 foot remnant of a younger surface into which the river

[1] A. A. Miller, op. cit., (1937), p. 158.
[2] Ibid, pp. 155-7.

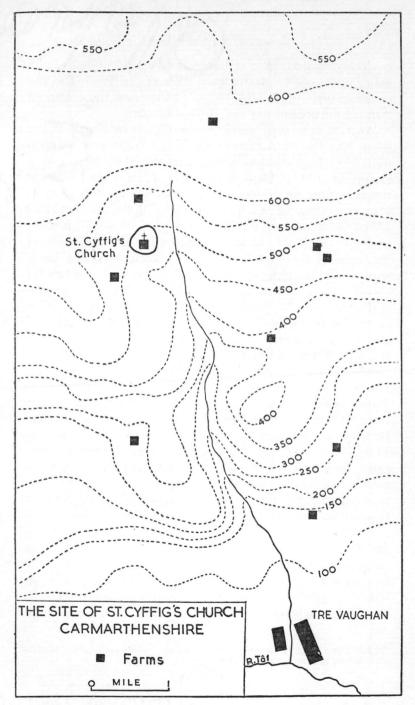

THE SITE OF ST. CYFFIG'S CHURCH
CARMARTHENSHIRE

■ Farms

MILE

TRE VAUGHAN

St. Cyffig's
Church

R. Tâf

Fig. 39

is deeply incised in a rejuvenation gorge. Finally, the valley opens out on to the flood-plain of the Taf. The site of the church (dedicated to St. Cyffig) and the scattered farms of the present day are also indicated.

We can now turn to similar evidence in North Wales where the Isle of Anglesey provides a convenient natural unit. We have already noted how the island was a very important cultural focus in the days of the saints, while at the same time we possess a fairly extensive knowledge of its geomorphology. The island, together with the adjacent Holy Island, is made up for the most part of pre-Cambrian crystalline rocks, but in spite of their great age and hardness the relief of the island is generally lowlying. The landscape comprises remnants of several former cycles of erosion which occurred when the sea-level was different from that of the present day. Each cycle resulted in the peneplanation or partial peneplanation of the island which was effected certainly in its later stages by marine erosion. Remnants of the former peneplains can be detected, one at 500 feet, another at 430 feet, and a third at various altitudes between 130 and 350 feet. The lowest and youngest peneplain, known as the Menai platform, is the most important of the three from the point of view of the present relief, as it covers between one half and a third of the total area of the island. From a height of about 350 feet in the north-west it slopes gently southwards and westward until it falls to approximately 130 feet above sea-level in the south-west.[1] We may consider 250 feet as a good average elevation, and so the contours for 250 feet and 50 feet respectively have been inserted on Fig. 40 to give a general indication of the tilted surface. It should be remembered that this platform has been, and is being, eroded by the present cycle and that the landscape has reached its greatest maturity in those areas where the platform is lowest, namely in the south-west. In the neighbourhood of the Menai Straits, recent (although

---

[1] Based on Greenly's *Geology of Anglesey*, op. cit. For a convenient summary see *The Land of Britain, Anglesey*, Part 34, 1940, pp. 215-21.

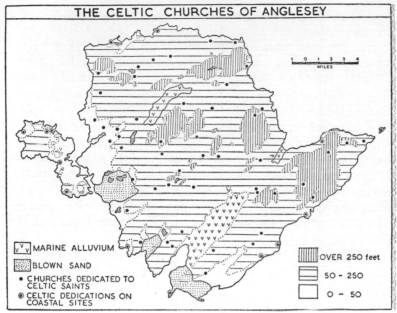

THE CELTIC CHURCHES OF ANGLESEY

MARINE ALLUVIUM
BLOWN SAND
• CHURCHES DEDICATED TO CELTIC SAINTS
⊚ CELTIC DEDICATIONS ON COASTAL SITES

OVER 250 feet
50 - 250
O - 50

Fig. 40

probably pre-Pleistocene) subsidence plays an important part in the evolution of the landscape. This is well shown in the river valleys with their deep trough-like sections near the coast, and the clear indications that adaptation to a new sea-level has not yet been reached in their upper portions, which consequently give all the appearances of a greater maturity. Superimposed on all this is a widespread mantle of boulder clay which fills up hollows, reduces the height of scraps and generally unifies the surface conditions. Extensive stretches of marine alluvium also exist, while in the south-west there are considerable areas of blown sand.

The sites of the sixty-seven churches and chapels on the island dedicated to the Celtic saints are marked on Fig. 40. Detailed examination has shown that fifty of these churches are sited not on the residual platform surfaces or on the valley floors but on the valley sides and, in particular, in the broad, upper sections of the valleys above the major ' knick-

point ' on the streams. As was the case on the borderlands of
Pembrokeshire and Carmarthenshire, we cannot illustrate
every site—we must be content with a single example—
Llandegfan, to the west of Beaumaris, in the south of the
island. Here, the Menai platform is approximately 300
ft. high and the remnants of its surface are shaded on Fig. 41.
Recent submergence in the Straits, as explained above, has
had its effect on the lower reaches of the Cadnant stream.
The contours numbered below 200 feet are closely packed
together, while the upper section of the valley shows signs
of greater maturity. St. Tegfan chose his site on a spur
overlooking the upper reaches of the valley. With local
modifications these conditions are repeated with great
frequency all over the island, as may be inferred generally
from Fig. 40.

Recent studies of the erosion surfaces of north Cardiganshire recognize not only high, middle and low plateau
surfaces but also a large number of sub-stages in the peneplanation of the area.[1] The rivers falling over this stair-
case of erosion surfaces, which ascends somewhat abruptly
from the coast, are naturally short and vigorous. Repeated rejuvenations have incised them deeply into the
general surface level. Such are the Leri, the Rheidol,
the Ystwyth and their tributaries. The process of oft-
repeated rejuvenation has left abundant evidence of previous
valley floors in the form of benches at different levels high
up on the present valley sides. Throughout most of this
north Cardiganshire region glacial erosion has also played
an important, but, as yet, uncalculated, part. Sufficient is
it to note the deepening of the valleys by ice action and the
wide-spread distribution of glacially produced land-forms
accompanied by the usual blanket of boulder clay. Most
of the valley benches, therefore, are almost certain to have
a thin veneer of drift on their surfaces. The Ystwyth and
Rheidol rivers have at the present time a relatively broad
and mature topography in their lower reaches, but their

---

[1] E. H. Brown, op. cit., (1950).

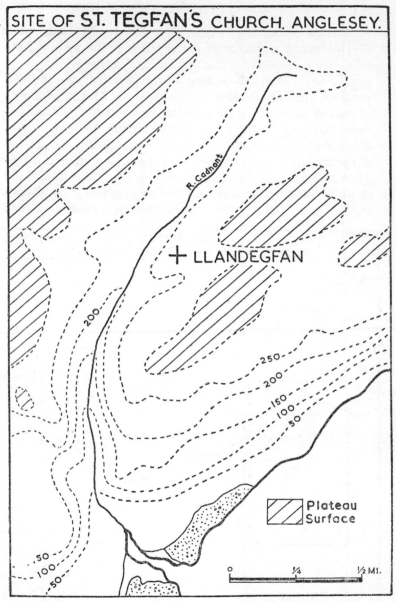

SITE OF **ST. TEGFAN'S** CHURCH. ANGLESEY.

R. Cadnant

+ LLANDEGFAN

200

250
200
150
100
50

50
100
50

Plateau
Surface

0   ¼   ½ MI.

Fig. 41

K

tributaries (especially where the main valley has been over-deepened by ice action) still fall into the main stream at a steep gradient. The presence of a flat valley floor results in a sharp slackening of the gradient for the still youthful tributary streams. This gives rise to the deposition of coarser material by the tributary rivers at their debouchement resulting in the formation of alluvial fans at a level above that of the major valley floor. Fig. 42 shows a portion of the middle Ystwyth valley between Llanafan and Llanilar while Figs. 43 and 44 show the detail of the sites of the churches of St. Ilar and St. Afan respectively. St. Afan's church is situated on the narrow neck of a clearly marked

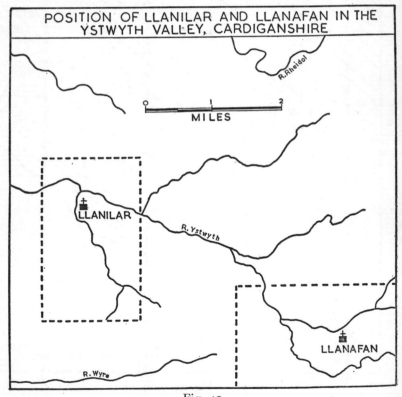

Fig. 42

bench in the Ystwyth valley. A tributary stream has
eroded itself through the bench to reach the main river, and
the later village by Llanafan has grown up in the narrow
valley of this tributary stream (Fig. 44). St. Ilar's church,
on the other hand, is well situated on one of the alluvial
fans formed by a swift flowing tributary of the Ystwyth.

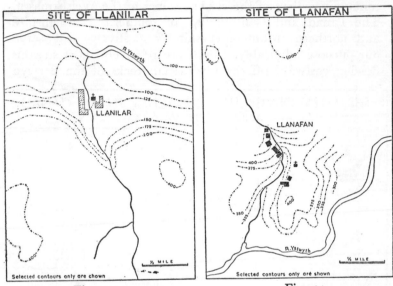

Fig. 43   Fig. 44

Selected contours at intervals of 25 feet show the steeply
graded stream, as well as the fine deltaic cone raised slightly
above the Ystwyth floor. The modern village of Llanilar
has gathered around the church. It should be remembered
that there are several such sites for Celtic churches in the
valleys of Wales ; that chosen by St. Padarn at Llanbadarn Fawr in the Rheidol valley provides another
example of a church on an alluvial fan within a few miles of
Llanilar. Alluvial cones provide not only areas of dry soil
set above the waters of the main stream, but also a means of
exit from the major valley by way of the tributary route—an
advantage not to be overlooked at a time when the broader
valley-ways had a forest cover with thick undergrowth.

A careful inspection of the physiography of the Welsh valleys indicates that river terraces, and glacial sands and gravels on the valley floor, offer attractive, dry sites in addition to those already mentioned. We have excellent examples of the utilization of such sites if we turn for illustration to some of the deep, steep sided, debris-choked, mountain valleys of the eastern slopes of the Welsh massif. The Tanad and Cain valleys of southern Denbighshire and northern Montgomeryshire respectively will serve our purpose admirably. Both are relatively short streams flowing eastward off the Ordovician rocks of the Berwyn

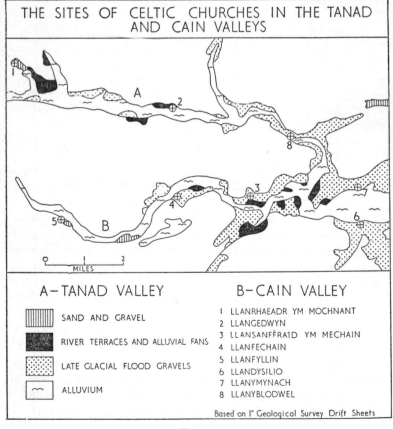

THE SITES OF CELTIC CHURCHES IN THE TANAD AND CAIN VALLEYS

A—TANAD VALLEY

SAND AND GRAVEL

RIVER TERRACES AND ALLUVIAL FANS

LATE GLACIAL FLOOD GRAVELS

ALLUVIUM

B—CAIN VALLEY

1 LLANRHAEADR YM MOCHNANT
2 LLANGEDWYN
3 LLANSANFFRAID YM MECHAIN
4 LLANFECHAIN
5 LLANFYLLIN
6 LLANDYSILIO
7 LLANYMYNACH
8 LLANYBLODWEL

Based on 1" Geological Survey Drift Sheets

Fig. 45

mountains. Both are deeply cleft into the upland mass. Glacial material of one sort or another is liberally spread over the whole countryside, eroded presumably by the former Berwyn ice-sheet. The valleys, in particular, are filled with masses of clay, sand and gravel, and there are also many evidences of the profound effect of glaciation on the drainage pattern, including the former occurrence of several extensive temporary lakes. Fig 45 ignores for the sake of clarity the widespread blanket of glacial boulder clay in these parts and shows merely the extraordinary complexity of the river terraces and the fluvio-glacial sand and gravel patches on the valley floors. It is possible, but by no means certain, that some of the river terraces may be pre-glacial in origin, but, even so, they all carry at the present time a veneer of glacial debris. In each of these narrow valley stretches are found three church sites originally established by the Celtic saints. In the Tanad valley there are Llan-rhaeadr-ym-Mochnant, Llangedwyn and Llanyblodwel, all carefully sited away from the narrow alluvial floor. The first named is on a patch of glacial sand, the second on a river terrace and Llanyblodwel on a patch of fluvio-glacial gravel. In the Cain valley we have Llanfyllin, Llanfechain and Llansanffraid ym Mechain. All three again avoid the alluvium. Llanfyllin is sited on boulder clay, Llan-fechain and Llansanffraid on fluvio-glacial gravels (see Fig. 45). To the eastward where the Efyrnwy from the south-west joins the drainage of this part of the Borderland we have two further examples of churches—Llandysilio and Llanymynach—clearly sited on the edge of fluvio-glacial gravel platforms raised above the valley floor. Examples of the utilization of similar sites by Celtic saints abound in other parts of Wales.

We have already indicated that while the examination of sites in the coastal and valley areas of Wales must be our major concern, those occurring in truly upland country must not be overlooked. There can be no doubt that a hill-site offered many attractions under certain circumstances to these wandering monks—their little cell might be the

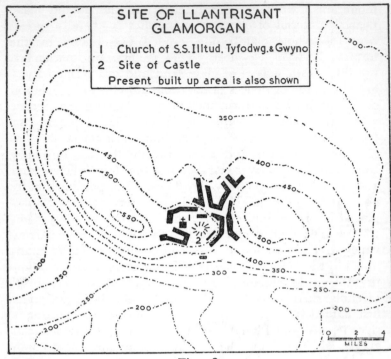

SITE OF LLANTRISANT GLAMORGAN

1   Church of S.S. Illtud, Tyfodwg, & Gwyno
2   Site of Castle
Present built up area is also shown

Fig. 46

symbol of the Eternal City ' set on a hill.'   Such sites occur
most frequently in the hill-country proper, above the valley-
ways and coastal margins.   Llantrisant on the southern
margins of the uplands of the South Wales coalfield in
Glamorgan may be cited as a typical example.   Fig. 46
shows a portion of the steep rim of the coal basin with two
neighbouring hills, 550 and 500 feet high respectively.
The Church of the Three Saints (Illtud, Gwyno and
Tyfodwg) is located on a projecting platform of the western-
most hill, in a strategic position sufficiently attractive to
entice a Norman castle in later times.   Similar sites are
frequent in the uplands, although prominent hills on the
lowland margins were often chosen, as, for example, at
Llangynnwr near Carmarthen;   Mathry in north Pembrokeshire, and Llandaniel-fab in Anglesey.

In conclusion it would appear that while the previous chapter has shown that the general distribution of the Celtic churches in Wales was closely bound up with cultural factors, the present chapter indicates that when individual sites are considered, local physical factors assume a predominant importance. It is possible to assign over forty per cent of the total number of Celtic churches to the upper, less rejuvenated sections of the Welsh valleys, another thirty-five per cent occupy sites on valley-benches, fluvioglacial debris and outwash cones ; twenty-two per cent are on coastal sites of different types, and the remainder on hill sites or in very specialized locations.

It is clear that the physical geography of Wales offered the Celtic saints a rich variety of possible sites for their settlements and that these opportunities were seized whenever they were required. It would be as absurd to be deflected from this argument by the fact that Celtic churches are not found on every island off the shore, or on every valley-bench, alluvial cone, river-terrace, hilltop or fluvioglacial gravel patch in Wales, as it would be to stress that Anglo-Saxon villages are not found along every spring-line in south-eastern England.

CHAPTER VIII

THE SETTLEMENT AROUND CELTIC CHURCHES — A STUDY OF FORM

W E are dependent on archaeological evidence for our knowledge of the form or lay-out of the settlements originally established by the Celtic saints, and we must admit at the outset that as far as Wales is concerned such evidence is meagre in the extreme. It is possible that the most frequent practice was for the churches and cells of the monks to be built of sods or of wattle and mud, and consequently no trace of them now remains. Only occasionally have rude stone structures been found, the foundations of which survive to give the archaeologist some picture of the lay-out of the original settlement.

No trace whatever has been found of the great monastic settlements that must have grown up at Llancarfan and Llanilltud Fawr, or in association with the traditional head-quarters of equally eminent saints such as Dyfrig, Dewi or Teilo. Likewise, in North Wales there are no traces of the famous monastery of Bangor-is-coed.[1] On the other hand, it would appear that something has survived of St. Seiriol's great monastery at Penmon in Anglesey. Here, a short distance from the medieval church (which is dedicated to the saint), are the ruins of a small rectangular chapel covering a holy well, alongside of which is an oval-shaped hut. These may well be the original buildings erected by St. Seiriol when he settled in the district.[2] It must also be borne in mind that the remains of the earliest settlements of the saints, if they survive at all, may now be beneath the medieval churches and their present church-yards. Excavations at St. Beuno's famous establishment at Clynnog

---

[1] A. E. Palmer, ' Notes on the Early History of Bangor-is-coed', *Y Cymmrodor*, Vol. X, 1889, pp. 14-15.

[2] Roy. Comm. Anc. Mont. *Anglesey*, pp. xci-xcii.

Fawr revealed that after his death a church built of stone was erected over the founder's tomb, as was frequently the custom in the Celtic church. When a later medieval church was erected, his bones were removed to a new building which became known as Eglwys y Bedd and there St. Beuno from his tomb continued to work miracles in the generations that followed.[1] The extensive archaeological work carried out in recent years in the neighbourhood of Illtud's famous monastery at Llanilltud Fawr, while indicating no traces of the traditional foundation of St. Illtud, nevertheless, proves that the field of search has been narrowed down to the ground more immediately contiguous to the church.[2] Such evidence, slight and inconclusive though it may be, gives added justification to the view adopted in this book that there is continuity of settlement on the site of existing churches from the days of the saints themselves.

It is generally agreed that such men as Cadog, Dewi, Teilo and Beuno established some fairly large monastic settlements with numerous buildings on their sites. Judging by the more extensive ruins of such settlements found in Ireland and in other areas outside Wales, the monks did not live in a large single building but in numerous scattered cells or groups of cells of the type uncovered at Nendrum in Northern Ireland,[3] or more recently by Mr. Ralegh Radford at Tintagel.[4] In addition to the church and monastic cells there would be the workrooms and graveyard of the community—the whole being enclosed by a wall or bank, or possibly by more than one such wall or bank.

The best preserved and, therefore, the best known Celtic monasteries, however, are the smaller houses or hermitages, normally located in secluded spots. The remains of such hermitages are common amongst the headlands and islands around the coasts of Scotland and Ireland. Many occurred

---

[1] B. Stallybrass, *Arch. Camb.*, 1914, pp. 271 and 292.

[2] See *Arch. Camb.*, 1915, p. 141; *Arch. Camb.*, 1937, p. 330 and *Bull. Board of Celtic Studies*, XIV, 1952, p. 313.

[3] C. A. Lawlor, *The Monastery of St. Mochaoi of Nendrum*, 1925.

[4] C. A. Ralegh Radford, 'Tintagel : The Castle and Celtic Monastery', *Ant. Journ.*, Vol. XV, No. 4, 1935.

in similar situations in Wales, but the archaeological
evidence is, once more, scanty. The Royal Commission
on Ancient Monuments in Wales give in their inventory for
the county of Anglesey a plan of such a hermitage as
revealed by excavation on Priestholm or Puffin Island.[1]

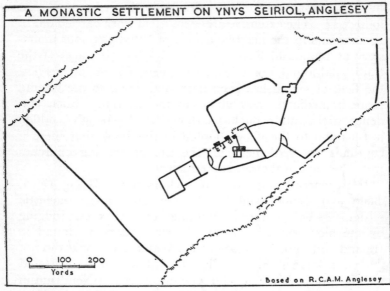

A MONASTIC SETTLEMENT ON YNYS SEIRIOL, ANGLESEY

0   100   200
Yards

Based on R.C.A.M. Anglesey

Fig. 47

This island lies about half a mile off the eastern end of
Anglesey and was known originally as Ynys Llannog and
later as Ynys Seiriol. The situation is typical of such
hermitages. The actual settlement is near the centre of
the tiny island. There remains a collapsed boundary wall,
not more than a foot high, forming a roughly oval enclosure
of about three-quarters of an acre around the church.
There are also the remains of three or four rectangular
cells grouped around the north-western part of the wall.
To the north and the northeast there are further enclosures,
while to the west of the main enclosure would appear to be
the remains of three smaller rectangular fields. (see Fig. 47).

[1] Roy. Comm. Anc. Mont. *Anglesey*, p. 143.

The site of the church is marked by a partly ruined central tower of twelfth century date. Excavation has shown the remains of a smaller, earlier church about five foot square, which was obviously rebuilt before the tower was placed against it in the twelfth century.[1] It is thought, however, that the remains of the earlier church are post-Viking in age, but they almost certainly replace a building of similar type. In this way we can trace successive churches on the original site founded by St. Seiriol (or one of his followers) and obtain some idea of the original plan of the whole settlement as it was in the seventh century. It is clear that the whole arrangement resembles a small farm or villa, and that the original church was never intended for large congregations, but was merely a place where the early Christian missionaries could worship. Such settlements as those on Priestholm never supported more than a few individuals and there is no evidence from archaeological or other sources of any contemporary secular settlement nearby. It should be noted, however, that the island site of Priestholm allowed the monks to set out a few small arable enclosures, but it is obvious from the sites of some of the monastic cells found in Ireland, Scotland and Wales that one anchorite alone must have dwelt in them and he must have lived by collecting wild fruit or by fishing or keeping a solitary cow, or more probably a goat, as the site by its rocky or precipitous character did not favour cultivation of any kind.

The important point for our general thesis is that nothing of the original lay-out of these settlements has survived into the modern settlement pattern of Wales. Sometimes, in other parts of the Celtic lands, as at Armagh in Northern Ireland, the plan of the present city shows in the lay-out of its streets the original oval boundary of the ' cashel ' or retaining walls by which the Celtic monastery, (that forms the nucleus of the settlement), was enclosed. In this instance the original Celtic church has become the present cathedral and it is most likely that the former retaining walls of the

[1] *Arch. Camb.*, 1901, p. 85.

monastic settlement were those of the native fort inside which the first Christian settlement was located. In most instances it is the church alone that continued to function when all other traces of the original monastery vanished, and when the customs and ritual of the Celtic church were superseded by those of Rome.

We must now turn to the secular settlements that gathered in later times around these ' church-points.' No one knows exactly the pattern of human settlement in Wales during the centuries contemporary with, and immediately following, the Age of the Saints, but the studies made in recent years by Professor T. Jones-Pierce and his colleagues of the legal and agrarian history of later periods allow us to make reasonable assumptions.[1] It would appear that the free tribesmen were originally, and presumably still at the time of the Celtic saints, semi-nomadic pastoralists who also practised a migratory tillage. They had temporary dwellings which could be easily constructed and moved. In selected areas of good agricultural land there would be the more permanent nucleated settlements of the non-free tribesmen who represented what remained of the earlier and, possibly, pre-Celtic inhabitants. Their economy had a stronger arable basis. Professor Jones-Pierce has shown that at various times between the ninth and the thirteenth centuries a gradual change took place whereby the free tribesmen settled down in more permanent dwellings. These dwellings were originally clustered together, but in later times there followed more and more dispersion leading up to the picture presented by our modern *tyddynnod*. Such a process was certainly going on in Anglesey and elsewhere in North Wales in the eleventh and twelfth centuries.[2]

As was indicated in a previous chapter there is some evidence to show that the larger monasteries of the Celtic church were located near to regions of contemporary dense

---

[1] See T. Jones-Pierce, ' Medieval Settlement in Anglesey', *Trans. Anglesey Ant. Soc.*, 1951, pp. 1-33 and G. R. J. Jones, ' Basic Patterns of Rural Settlement in North Wales', *Inst. of British Geographers Transactions*, No. 19, 1953.

[2] T. Jones-Pierce, op. cit., *Trans. Ang. Ant. Soc.*, 1951.

population. This would mean that they were near to regions where the non-free tribesmen had settled on relatively good agricultural land. The hermitage type of settlement, so frequently established by the Celtic saints, bore, as we have seen, little relationship to the contemporary settlement pattern, and even after the little churches were rebuilt and used for congregational worship as was the Roman custom of later times, the church itself tended to emerge as an isolated structure in the medieval settlement pattern.

Dr. Emrys Jones has recently taken the story a stage further and pursued the matter down to the study of present-day settlement conditions. He sees the gradually extending tribal lands of the Dark and Middle Ages, wherein the free tribesmen were settling, expanding so as to include forest-land on the better portions of the lower hill-slopes. Such an expansion would frequently take into its bounds a holy site or cell that was previously isolated. Dr. Jones applies the term *treflan* to such a settlement of free tribesmen (traditionally referred to as a *tref*) engulfing a former Celtic church (*llan*).[1] He has been able to pick out on the modern Ordnance Survey maps several of these *treflannau* in the Teifi valley in Cardiganshire and north Carmarthenshire—an area which he has studied in detail. He is convinced that in this area the church has had no nucleating influence whatsoever. Sometimes, however, he can detect a slight focusing around the inn, school or vicarage which may be accentuated if the *treflan* is on a main road, but generally he finds the church itself almost as isolated as any one of the scattered farms. Its main function has been to give unity to minor neighbourhoods which have no other outward expression of their social cohesion.[2] The overall picture, therefore, is that nucleation of settlement around a Celtic church is normally very restricted, or almost non-existent, except where nodality has in very special cases

[1] E. Jones, 'Settlement patterns in the Middle Teifi Valley', *Geography*, No. 150, Vol. XXX, Pt. 4, 1945, p. 109.

[2] E. Jones, 'Some aspects of the study of Settlement in Britain', *The Advancement of Science*, No. 29, Vol. III, 1951, p. 62.

sharply accentuated its development.[1] Prior to Dr. Jones'
study of the settlements of the Teifi valley, Mr. Robert
Richards had made a similar observation regarding the
ancient churches of Ardudwy. After pointing out how the
churches of this part of Merioneth with a single exception,
are all within sight of the sea, Mr. Richards observes that
they all stand without settlement near at hand. Llandecwyn stands aloof with (significantly) *Ty'n llan* as its
sole companion. The same is true of Llanfrothen, while
Llandannwg, also, had only one house *Ty'n-y-maes*, in
its immediate neighbourhood until quite recently.[2] Indeed, it is abundantly clear from the foregoing statements
that the chief characteristic of the Celtic churches is the
isolated position occupied by a very large number of them
in the settlement pattern of rural Wales down to present
times.

No one has, however, attempted an appraisal of the extent
to which this generalization is true for Wales as a whole.
Such work can only be done by an examination of each
individual site and the production of a statistical summary.
The card catalogue of the Celtic churches in Wales prepared
for this work and already mentioned in the Introduction,
included for each church a note based on the 1 :25,000 sheets
regarding the present extent of nucleation around the
church. The catalogue, therefore, provides a basis for
such an appraisal and an attempt has been made to group
the data so that we have four categories of generally increasing intensity of settlement, beginning with those
churches with virtually no nucleation around them, and
ending with those around which urban or semi-urban
settlements (judged by their size alone) have gathered.

The first category is clearly the most significant. Within
it are considered not only the instances where the church is
absolutely by itself but also such minute nucleations as

[1] E. Jones, op. cit., *Geography*, 1945, 109.
[2] R. Richards, ' Ardudwy and its ancient Churches,' *Harlech Studies*, presented
to Dr. Thomas Jones, C. H., Edited B. B. Thomas (University of Wales Press,
1938), p. 175.

occur when a vicarage or rectory together with a single farm are found alongside. As we have seen this simple pattern is often met with in the Welsh countryside, and there is much evidence to show that such an arrangement frequently occurred in the past. It is not easy to obtain direct carto-graphical evidence of it in the past, largely because prior to the Tithe Maps and the first edition of the Ordnance Survey in the early nineteenth century, there are no maps that, on the one hand, cover the Principality as a whole and, on the other, are of a sufficiently large scale to show individual buildings. Wales, however, is fortunate in that Edward Lhwyd—the second Keeper of the Ashmolean Museum in Oxford—in the early years of the eighteenth century conceived the idea of producing a geographical gazetteer of his native land. He collected his information by means of a questionnaire addressed to the vicar or rector of every parish in the Principality which asked, among other things, for details of the number of houses and their geographical distribution within the respective parishes. Alas, not every incumbent returned his form and many, doubtless, found the task too great, but the fragmentary material that was assembled has been published as supplementary volumes by the Cambrian Archaeological Association and is known as Lhwyd's *Parochialia*.[1] The entry for Llanbadarn Fawr in Radnorshire shows that at the close of the seventeenth century this settlement must have appeared very much as it does today (Fig. 48), for the vicar of that time states that there is 'no town or village only 2 houses by ye church'.[2] Similar entries abound ; at Llanwnws in Cardiganshire there was ' 1 house by church called Pentre,'[3] while at Capel Garmon, near Llanrwst in Denbighshire the rector reported ' but 2 houses there are by Capel Garmon,'[4] and even at St. Petrox in English speaking Pembrokeshire there was ' no

---

[1] R. H. Morris (Edit.) Edward Lhwyd *Parochialia*, Cambrian Archaeological Association, Supplements 1909, 1910 and 1911.

[2] Ibid., III, 93.

[3] Ibid., III, 74.

[4] Ibid., I, 15.

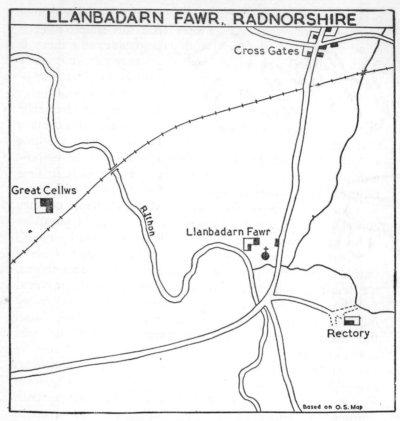

Fig. 48 (Scale 1″ = ¼ mile)

market town &c., there being only one house (which is the rector's) near the church.'[1]   It would appear, therefore, that the pattern of settlement around the Celtic church as described for Merioneth by Mr. Richards was very much in evidence all over Wales two hundred and fifty years ago. Out of the 614 sites examined for the whole of Wales on the present Ordnance Survey Sheets, 268 of them, that is forty-four per cent, fall into this category.   As this is the *most* (although by no means, as previous workers have

---

[1] Ibid., III, 5.

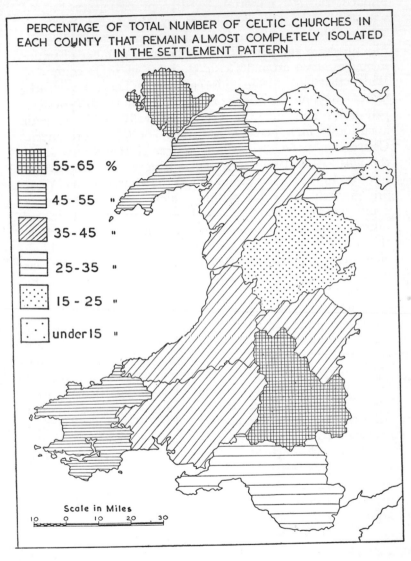

PERCENTAGE OF TOTAL NUMBER OF CELTIC CHURCHES IN EACH COUNTY THAT REMAIN ALMOST COMPLETELY ISOLATED IN THE SETTLEMENT PATTERN

55-65 %
45-55 "
35-45 "
25-35 "
15-25 "
under 15 "

Scale in Miles
10   0   10   20   30

Fig. 49

L

implied, the *all*) important settlement pattern associated with sites originally established by the Celtic saints in Wales, a study of its overall distribution pattern is indicated. Fig. 49 shows the percentage of the total number of settlements gathered around Celtic churches in each county of Wales that fall within this category. They are clearly most numerous in the north-western and south-western peninsulas and in west Wales generally, coupled with a curiously high percentage in the county of Brecknock. Conversely, along the eastern borders of Wales and along the northern and southern coastal fringes there appears to have been more nucleation around the churches, and these are precisely the areas within which such developments could have been expected to have taken place both on historical and on economic grounds. Thus, we can conclude that the Celtic churches have remained relatively isolated elements in the settlement pattern of Wales in those areas where two factors have operated together, namely, that the area in question was originally thickly planted with Celtic cells (as was shown to be the case in the north-west and south-west peninsulas, and also in south-east Wales (including Brecknockshire), and where subsequent economic development was such as not to attract any considerable influx of population. These factors operate in Atlantic Wales generally, while Brecknockshire stands clearly apart from Glamorgan and western Monmouthshire in not participating in the industrial influx of population that characterized those areas. Outstanding, therefore, is the fact that over much of Wales the Celtic saints established many more potential nuclei of settlement than the cultural and economic life of the community has been able to develop in subsequent times. That the settlement pattern is ill-adjusted to the potentialities of the physical environment is a well-known feature of rural Wales.[1]

We have now set the stage, and, indeed, put forward the

---

[1] Note, for example, the large number of railway junctions with no settlement whatever around them : Dyfi Junction, Three Cocks Junction, Afon Wen Junction, Moat Lane Junction, etc.

basic considerations which should guide our study of the
remaining forms of nucleation around the Celtic churches.
The second category in our fourfold classification is represented by the present conditions at Llanwyddelan in north-
eastern Montgomeryshire. Here we see a minor hamlet
of some nine or ten houses associated with the church. The

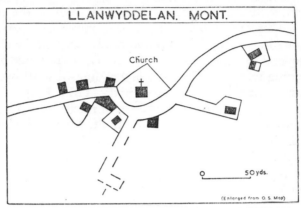

LLANWYDDELAN. MONT.

Church

50 yds.

(Enlarged from O. S. Map)

Fig. 50

nodal character of the settlement is clearly emphasized by
the close relationship of the houses to the road. The latter
is certainly later than the church as it curves markedly
around it. (Fig. 50). The rector of Llanwyddelan does
not appear to have made a return to Edward Lhwyd, and so
we are not certain of the number of houses around the
church at the close of the seventeenth century. Nevertheless, Lhwyd's incomplete returns contain numerous references
to tiny hamlets of this kind gathered about Celtic churches
all over Wales. At Marchwiail (dedicated to St. Deiniol)
in north-eastern Wales, we are told that ' By ye church are
5 houses and a little smithie.'[1] St. Illtud's northern out-
post at Llanelltud in Merioneth had ' 5 houses by church,'[2]
while the vicar of Llanuwchllyn reported ' 9 ty wrth yr
Eglwys.'[3] Calculated from the present Ordnance Survey

[1] Lhwyd, op. cit., I, 136.
[2] Ibid., I. 1.
[3] Ibid., II. 70. (Trans. ' 9 houses by the Church ').

sheets there would appear to be 135 examples out of a total
of 614 (22 per cent) that could be included within this
category.

The next category may be termed the church village.
Here we find a substantial nucleation amounting to possibly
thirty or forty houses clustered neatly around the church.
Frequently, the Celtic church stands by itself at the centre
of the settlement with either an open space or a roadway
encircling it.   A number of radial roads focus on the church
from several directions and the homesteads are found in the
intervening sectors.   The plan of Pendine in south-western
Carmarthenshire as it appears on the Tithe Map of 1842
is clearly representative of this form of nucleation (Fig. 51).
The church is at present dedicated to St. Margaret Marloes,
but this is a medieval replacement of an original Teilo
dedication.   Nucleations of this rather substantial, compact
type seem to have been fairly widely distributed in certain
parts of Wales in pre-industrial times.   Lhwyd's correspond-

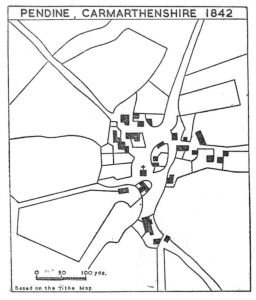

Fig. 51

ent at Cadoxton-by-Neath in Glamorgan reported that
' It has a fair village by ye church,'[1] while at Llandrillo in
Merioneth there were ' 30 houses by ye church.'[2] The
latter village, less disturbed than Cadoxton in modern times,
still preserves a form like that of Pendine in 1842. It is
significant that such a pattern appears in somewhat modified
form associated with many of the famous sites in Celtic
hagiology. Llanilltud Fawr, Llancarfan, Mathry in north
Pembrokeshire, Llanddewibrefi and Llanbadarn Fawr in
Cardiganshire, Llangynog in Montgomeryshire[3] are all
fundamentally of this type. An examination of the present
day Ordnance Survey sheets records 55 examples of this
kind of nucleation in Wales as a whole, representing
approximately nine per cent of the total number of Celtic
church sites known to exist.

It is worth while noting with reference to this particular
type of settlement that previous workers in their enthusiasm
to classify settlement types on form alone, without adequate
reference to historical evidence, have claimed the church-
village, described herewith, as a distinct type of its own,
especially when it occurs on the crest of a hill as at Mathry.
Some have even seen in such villages, when the ancient
church-yard wall is roughly circular in plan, a connection
between these settlements and the Megalithic culture which
left such a deep impression on the Atlantic fringes of our
islands.[4] Such speculation would appear to be entirely
unwarranted, and we prefer to see no more in this type of
rural settlement than a simple nucleation of houses around
the ancient church which happens to have proceeded, owing
to local nodal facilities, a few stages beyond that shown in
our categories I and II, and not far enough to reach urban
or even semi-urban status. The fact that an examination

---

[1] Ibid., III, 68.

[2] Ibid., II. 56.

[3] See the plan of this village based on the Terrier of 1775 in Robert Richards,
Cymru'r Oesau Canol, (Wrecsam, 1933), p. 68.

[4] See *Geographical Teacher* 1926, pp. 317-324 ; and *Geographical Journal*,
Vol. CX, 1947, pp. 76-93.

of the full evidence for Wales shows that these church-villages occur on a great variety of sites, and are most numerous in the eastern and southern counties (see county lists on p. 159) provides but a slender basis for the investigator who seeks to afford them any peculiar siting or distributional significance. The simple explanation is that they represent a stage in the intensity of nucleation found in association with Celtic churches.

We have already indicated that a further increase in the amount of nucleation would tend to place the settlements in an urban or semi-urban category, at least from the point of view of size. As is well known, size alone, in Wales, is no criterion of urban status. History and function are both important considerations. The true town was exotic in Wales and came in under Norman influence. In some cases, as at Carmarthen the new Norman town was placed alongside the old settlement gathered around the cell of a famous saint. Old and New Carmarthen were thus separate entities down to the sixteenth century. In other cases, a Norman borough supplanted the settlement around the church as, for example, at Monmouth ; at other times, the town was a *de novo* creation, as at Aberystwyth; while at the same time many of the original nuclei around Celtic churches have continued to grow in size (especially in modern times) and so to assume urban functions. The extent of their growth depends on the richness of the hinterland and whether it provides a rural or an industrial background. Such are the settlements with which we are directly concerned in this analysis. Approximately 156 settlements of this type (about one quarter of the total associated with Celtic churches) are known to exist in Wales. The list would include towns of such varied sizes as Tregaron (pop. 600), Llandeilo (1,800), Holyhead (10,700), Holywell (3,420), Hawarden (5,370) and Llanelly (38,390) and would be capable of considerable subdivision if this were thought necessary.

Some of these settlements had already grown to reasonable size in pre-industrial times. Lhwyd's data for Flintshire are fairly complete and his correspondents tell us that at the close of the seventeenth century Hawarden was ' a village containing about 60 houses '[1] while Holywell was even then ' a town of about 120 houses.'[2] When the growth of such settlements has been relatively small it is still possible to distinguish the original nucleus, together with the subsequent stages of growth,[3] but in those where growth has been rapid and haphazard, as in the case of the industrial settlements, this is not always easy. In fact, the resultant pattern formed by the built-up area is often entirely fortuitous. For illustrative purposes, therefore, it is well to select a settlement like Llandysilio in Montgomeryshire where the process has proceeded beyond the nucleations typical of our categories I and II, and has not developed on lines typical of category III, but yet shows that the inital steps towards category IV have already taken place. The location of the original settlement of St. Tysilio is clearly seen with the usual " five or six houses around the church " as is typical of settlements in our category II, but, as seems to have been frequently the case, St. Tysilio placed his little cell almost alongside the Roman road. Such roads continued to be used as trackways for generations afterwards and in this case both the 18th century and the present-day road follow the Roman routeway. With the increased use of such roads in the early nineteenth century this particular section began to carry heavy traffic between north and south. New buildings were erected, shops, inns and a smithy together with many others that gathered the profit of the road. Some of the dwellings such as Street Farm and Street Cottage are significantly named. The road was later followed by the railway which, as shown on Fig. 52, runs parallel to it. Then came the station, and later, a school and two non-conformist chapels, and now a large motor garage.

---

[1] Lhwyd, Ibid., I, 93.
[2] Ibid., I, 71.
[3] E. Jones, ' Tregaron—a Welsh market town', *Geography*, No. 167, Vol. XXXV, Pt. I, 1950, pp. 20-21.

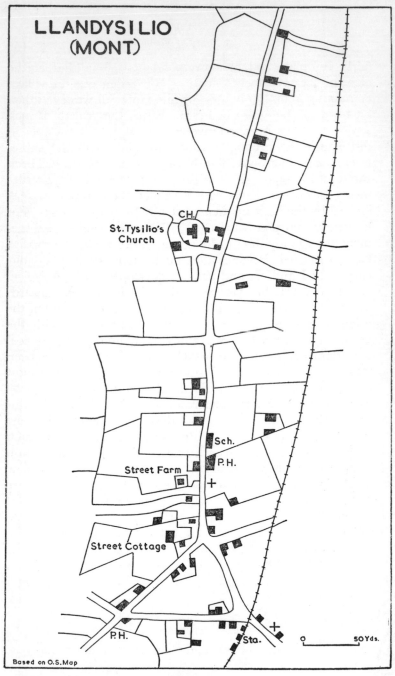

Fig. 52

It would appear that a modern focus is gathering near to a road island south of St. Tysilio's original site. Nevertheless, this embryo-town (for such it is, rather than a village community gathered together for agricultural purposes) continues to bear the name of the Celtic saint, and shows clearly the process of accretion towards urban status.

Finally, it should be noted that the extent of nucleation near any given church varies considerably with time. For example, it could remain relatively static as at Llangynllo in Cardiganshire or at Llanbadarn Fawr in Radnorshire, or, on the contrary, settlements that would be included within category I at the end of the seventeenth century, or at the beginning of the nineteenth century, may be found in any of the other categories today. Thus, Lhwyd's correspondent stated of Llysfaen in Caernarvonshire (whose church is dedicated to St. Cynfran) ' Nid oes ond day dy neu dri wrth yr Eglwys' (' There are only two or three houses by the church')[1] yet, with the development of slate quarrying, Llysfaen today represents a nucleation of category IV type. Such examples can clearly be multiplied on the South Wales coalfield. On the other hand, the reverse process has occurred, particularly in association with rural depopulation in the nineteenth century. Figs. 53a and 53b show the extent of depopulation around Cilrhedyn church on the borders of Carmarthenshire and Pembrokeshire. The first map shows the position in 1841 (based on the Tithe Map of that date) and the second map, the position as it is today. The church is dedicated to no less a personage than St. Teilo. In 1841 the settlement would fall within our category II but present day conditions show it as an excellent example of category I.

We have illustrated the many pitfalls that beset the geographer who attempts to classify settlements according to the pattern they form on the current sheets of the Ordnance Survey, yet when *extent* of nucleation about a pivot rather than *pattern* is involved there is much to be

[1] Lhwyd, Ibid., I, 39.

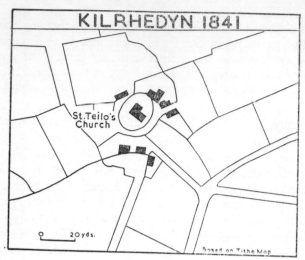

Fig. 53A

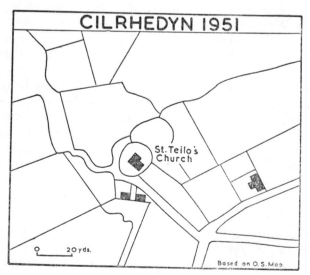

Fig. 53B

revealed by the analysis made in this chapter of *all* the
settlements gathered around the known Celtic churches in
Wales today.   The table below gives a statistical summary
on a county basis for the country as a whole.

There are below points worthy of note.   In the first
place there is no evidence of any significant regional or
cultural pattern in any of the four categories under review,

SETTLEMENT CATEGORIES

County	Category I.	Category II.	Category III.	Category IV.	Total
Anglesey	45	11	1	11	68
Brecknock	25	9	5	6	45
Caernarvon	22	11	3	13	49
Cardigan	17	11	4	12	44
Carmarthen	24	11	5	22	62
Denbigh	14	9	7	15	45
Flint	1	3	3	7	14
Glamorgan	18	16	9	21	64
Merioneth	9	5	2	7	23
Monmouth	20	14	—	8	42
Montgomery	8	5	8	13	34
Pembroke	45	13	6	18	82
Radnor	11	11	2	2	26
Hereford	9	6	—	1	16
Totals	268	135	55	156	614
Per Cent.	44	22	9	25	100

except, perhaps, for the fact that churches with little or no
settlement around them (Category I) are certainly more
numerous in the extreme north-western and south-western
peninsulas of the country than elsewhere.   The explanation
of this distribution has already been given and it remains
only to draw attention to the fact that the highest percentage of churches with no nucleation around them occurs
in the lowlying parts of Wales and not in the uplands where,
on *a priori* grounds it might be expected.   Pembrokeshire
and Anglesey are the two counties of lowest relief in the
Principality.

The number of settlements in categories I and II, taken
together total 403 and thereby far outnumber the combined
totals of categories III and IV (211).   The same dominance

of categories I and II over III and IV can be traced in each county of Wales and the Borderland with the exception of Flint and Montgomery. The conclusion, thus, is inescapable that the Celtic churches, as such, did not possess great nucleating power in the settlement pattern of Wales, although it would be a considerable overstatement to maintain that they had none. This general conclusion is understandable when we recall that the Celtic church was in origin a cell, most frequently a hermit's cell, specially sited away from the main lines of human movement. The church did not originate as a ' settlement' or as a centre of population, however small,—it only became such if later economic development found it a pivot conveniently located ; even then it had to compete in Wales with well-positioned urban pivots established and nurtured by alien influence.

In conclusion, it should be stressed that any classification of settlement around the Celtic churches as attempted here is largely a matter of convenience. It does not permit the drawing of too many general conclusions. The geographer must study the site, position, function and form of each settlement individually, and realize that such work cannot begin until the original emplacement is thoroughly understood. It is towards such an understanding that this book has been written.

BIBLIOGRAPHY

The following bibliography does not claim to be complete. It does not cover all aspects of the Lives of the Saints or the story of the Celtic Church in Wales, neither does it provide a complete list of works on the prehistory or the settlement pattern of Wales. It includes simply those writings which have been used in the preparation of this work and is divided into primary sources, studies, and articles for the sake of convenience.

I. PRIMARY SOURCES

Dimock, J. F. (Edit.), Giraldus Cambrensis *Itinerarium Kambriae et Descriptio Kambriae*, London, 1908.

Evans, J. G. and Rhys J. (Editors) *Liber Landavensis*. The text of the Book of Llan Dav. Oxford, 1893.

Evans, J. G. (Edit.) *The Book of Taliesin* 'Arymes Prydein Vawr,' Oxford, 1910.

Griscom, A. (Edit.) *Historia Regum Britanniae* (Geoffrey of Monmouth), London, 1929.

Grosjean, P. (Edit.) *Acta Sanctorum*. A travers trois siècles. L'ouvre des Bollandistes, 1615-1915. Bruxelles, 1920.

Gwynn, J. (Edit.) *Beati Martini Vita*. (Sulpicius Severus) Royal Irish Academy, 1913.

Hornis, G. (Edit.) *Sulpicii Severi Presbyteri Opera Omnia*, London, 1665.

Jones, J. Morris and Rhys, J. (Editors) *Llyvyr Ankyr Llandewivrevi*, Oxford, 1894.

Le Grand, Albert (Edit.) *Les vies des saints de la Bretágne Armoriques*, Quimper, 1901.

Macalister, R. A. S. *Corpus Inscriptionum Insularum Celticarum*, Vols, I and II., Dublin, 1945-49.

Morris, R. H. (Edit.) *Parochialia*, (Edward Lhwyd) Cambrian Archaeological Association Supplements, 1909-11.

Nash-Williams, V. E. *The Early Christian Monuments of Wales*. Cardiff, 1950.

O'Hanlon, J. (Edit.) *Lives of the Irish Saints*. Dublin, 1875 ff.

Owen, H. (Edit.) *The Description of Pembrokeshire* (George Owen) 4 Parts. Cymmrodorion Record Series, No. I. London, 1892-1936.

Rees, William, *An Historical Atlas of Wales*. Cardiff, 1951.

Rees, W. J. (Edit.) *Lives of the Cambro-British Saints*. Welsh Mss Society, 1853.

Stevenson, W. H. (Edit.) *Life of Alfred* (Asser), Oxford, 1904.

Toulmin-Smith, L. (Edit.) *Itinerary* (J. Leland), I-V, 1907-10.

Wade-Evans, A. W. (Edit.) *Vitae Sanctorum Britanniae et Genealogiae*, Cardiff, 1944.

Williams, H. (Edit.) *De Excidio Britanniae* (Gildas) Fragmenta, Liber de Paenitentia accedit et Lorica Gildae, Cymmrodorion Record Series, No. 3, London, 1899-1901.

Year Book of The Church in Wales, Cardiff, (Annual).

Royal Commission on Ancient and Historic Monuments in Wales and Monmouthshire. Inventories : *Montgomery* (1911) ; *Flint* (1912) ; *Radnor* (1913) ; *Denbigh* (1914) ; *Carmarthen* (1917) ; *Merioneth* (1921) ; *Pembroke* (1925) ; *Anglesey* (1937).

Maps : Ordnance Survey ;   1" to 1 mile original edition (with Mss. Field
Survey 2" to 1 mile) 1820-1830 ; Six inches to 1 mile : 1 : 25,000 2nd
Provisional edition, 1941-43.   *Ordnance Survey map of Roman Britain,*
1:1,000,000 (1928).   *Ordnance Survey Map of Britain in the Dark Ages* (south
sheet) 1 : 1,000,000 (1935).   Geological survey of England and Wales
1" to 1 mile, (Solid and Drift sheets where available). W. Rees, *Map*
of South Wales in the fourteenth Century, ½ inch to 1 mile. Cardiff, 1936.
Ordnance Survey Map of XVII Century England. 1 : 1,000,000. (1930).
Tithe Commutation Maps on parish basis, approximately 12 inches
to 1 mile. 1836-1848.

II. STUDIES

Baring-Gould S. and Fisher, J. *The Lives of the British Saints.*   4 Vols. London,
1907-13.
Bury, J. B. *The Life of St. Patrick and his place in History*, London, 1905.
Chadwick, Nora K. (Ed.) *Studies in Early British History*, Cambridge, 1954.
Charlesworth, M. P. *The Lost Province.* Cardiff, 1949.
Collingwood, R. G. and Myres, J. N. L. *Roman Britain and the English Settle-*
ments. Oxford, 1936.
Doble, G. H. The ' Cornish Saints' Series,' Nos. 1-48.   1923-1944.
Doble, G. H. The ' Welsh Saints' Series ' Nos. 1-5.   1942-44.
Doble, G. H. *Saint Iltut.* Cardiff, 1944.
Duke, J. A. *The Columbian Church.* Oxford, 1936.
Fawtier, R. *La Vie de Saint Sampson.* Paris, 1912.
Fox, Sir Cyril. *The Personality of Britain.* 4th Edition. Cardiff, 1943.
Fox, Sir Cyril. *A find of the Early Iron Age from Llyn Cerrig Bach, Anglesey.* Cardiff,
1946.
Gougaud, Dom. L. *Christianity in Celtic Lands.* London, 1932.
Greenly, E. *The Geology of Anglesey.* H.M.S.O. 2 Vols. 1919.
Grimes, W. F. *Guide to the Collections illustrating the Prehistory of Wales* (National
Museum of Wales). Cardiff, 1939.
Hencken, H. O'N. *Archaeology of Cornwall and Scilly.* London, 1932.
Hughes, H. and North, H. L. *The Old Churches of Snowdonia.* Bangor, 1924.
Jackson, K. *Language and History in Early Britain*, Edinburgh, 1953.
James, J. W. *A Church History of Wales.* London, 1945.
Jones, Francis, *The Holy Wells of Wales*, Cardiff, 1954.
Jones, G. Hartwell. ' Celtic Britain and the Pilgrim Movement.'   *Y Cym-*
mrodor, XXIII.   1912.
Kinvig, R. H. *A History of the Isle of Man.* Liverpool, 1950.
Largillière, J. *Les Saints et l'organisation chretienne primitive dans l'Armorique*
Bretonne. Rennes, 1925.
Lawlor, H. C. *The Monastery of St. Mochaoi of Nendrum.* Belfast, 1925.
Lewis, H. *Datblygiad Yr Iaith Gymraeg.* Caerdydd, 1931.
Lloyd, Sir John E. (Edit.) *A History of Carmarthenshire.* Vol. I. Cardiff, 1935.
Lloyd, Sir John E. *A History of Wales*, Vols. I and II, 3rd Edit. London, 1939.
Loth, J. *Les Noms des Saints Bretons.* Paris, 1910.
Mackinder, Sir H. J. *Britain and the British Seas.* Oxford, 1905.
Peake, H. and Fleure, H. J. *The Corridors of Time*, Vols. I-IX. Oxford, 1927-
1936.
Rees, R. *An Essay on the Welsh Saints.* London, 1836.
Richards, R. *Cymru'r Oesau Canol.* Wrecsam, 1933.
Simpson, W. D. *The Celtic Church in Scotland.*   Aberdeen University Studies,
No. III.   1935.
Steers, J. A. *The Coastline of England and Wales.* Cambridge, 1946.
Stenton, Sir F. M. *Anglo-Saxon England.* Oxford, 1943.

Taylor, T. *The Life of St. Samson of Dol.* London, 1925.
Thomas. R. J. *The Brychan Dynasty in East Glamorgan.* Cardiff, 1936.
Wade-Evans, A. W. *Life of St. David.* London, 1923.
Wade-Evans, A. W. *Welsh Christian Origins.* Oxford, 1934.
Williams, Hugh. *Christianity in Early Britain.* Oxford, 1912.
Williams, Sir Ifor. *Canu Aneirin.* Caerdydd, 1938.
Williams, Sir Ifor. *Enwau Lleoedd.* (Cyfres Pobun, V). Lerpwl, 1945.
Zimmer, H. *The Celtic Church in Britain and Ireland.* Trans. by A. Meyer. London, 1902.

III. ARTICLES

Baillie-Reynolds, P. K. 'The Roman Occupation of North Wales', *Trans. Anglesey Ant. Soc. and Field Club*, 1932-33.
Bersu, G. and Griffiths, W. E. 'Concentric Circles at Llwyn-du Bach, Peny-groes', *Caernarvonshire Arch. Soc.*, Vol. C, 1949.
Bowen, E. G. 'A Study of Rural Settlements in South-west Wales', *Geographical Teacher*, XIII, 1926.
Bowen, E. G. 'The Travels of the Celtic Saints', *Antiquity*, XVIII, 1944.
Bowen, E. G. 'The Settlements of the Celtic Saints in South Wales', *Antiquity*, XIX, 1945.
Bowen, E. G. 'The Saints of Gwynedd', *Trans. Caern. Hist. Soc.*, 1948.
Bowen, E. G. 'The Celtic Saints in Cardiganshire', *Ceredigion*, I, 1950.
Brooke, G. C. 'The Distribution of Gaulish and British Coins in Britain,' *Antiquity*, VII, 1933.
Brown, E. H. 'Erosion Surfaces in North Cardiganshire', *Trans. and Papers Inst. of British Geographers*, No. 16, 1950.
Crawford, O. G. S. 'Western Seaways' in *Custom is King*, Oxford, 1936.
Doble, G. H. 'The Relics of St. Petroc', *Antiquity*, XXI, 1939.
Doble, G. H. 'St. Congar', *Antiquity*, XIX, 1945.
Emanuel, H. D. 'The Latin "Life" of St. Cadoc : A Textual and Lexicographical Study', M.A. thesis of the University of Wales, Mss, 1950.
Fisher, J. 'Welsh Church Dedications', *Trans. Hon. Soc. Cymmrod.*, XV, 1906-07.
Fox, Aileen. 'Early Welsh Homesteads on Gelligaer Common, Glamorgan', *Archaeologia Cambrensis*, XCIV, 1939.
Fox, Aileen. 'The Siting of some Inscribed Stones of the Dark Ages in Glamorgan and Breconshire', *Archaeologia Cambrensis*, XCIV, 1939.
Fox, Aileen. 'Early Christian Period', *A Hundred Years of Welsh Archaeology*, Cambrian Archaeological Association, 1846-1946.
Fox, Sir Cyril. 'An Encrusted Urn of the Bronze Age', *Antiquaries Journal*, VII, 1927.
Fox, Sir Cyril and Aileen. 'Platform house-sites of South-Wales type in Swydd Buddugre, Malienydd, Radnorshire', *Archaeologia Cambrensis*, C, 1948.
Fox, G. E. and Hope, W. H. St. J. 'Excavations on the Site of the Roman City of Silchester, Hants, in 1893', *Archaeologia*, LIV, 1894.
Fox, Sir C. and Hyde, H. A. 'A Second Cauldron and an Iron Sword from the Llyn Fawr Hoard', *Antiquaries Journal*, XIX, 1939.
Graham, T. H. B. and Collingwood, W. G. 'Patron Saints of the Diocese of Carlisle', *Trans. Cumb. and Westmorland Ant. and Arch. Soc.*, 1925.
Grosjean, P. 'Notes d'hagiographie celtique', *Analecta Bollandiana*, LXIII, 1945.
Grosjean, P. 'S. Paterne d'Avranches et S. Paterne de Vannes dan les anciens martyrologes', *Analecta Bollandiana*, LXVII, 1949.
Grosjean, P. 'Bulletin des Publications Hagiographiques', *Analecta Bollandiana*, LXIX, 1951.

Hemp, W. J. and Gresham, C. A. 'Hut Circles in North Wales', *Antiquity*, XVIII, 1944.

Hogg, A. H. A. 'The Date of Cunedda', *Antiquity*, XXII, 1948.

Hogg, A. H. A. 'The Votadini' in *Aspects of Archaeology in Britain and Beyond*, London, 1951.

Hughes, H. 'Ynys Seiriol', *Archaeologia Cambrensis*, New Series I, 1901.

Hunter-Blair, P. 'The Origins of Northumbria', *Archaeologia Aeliana*, XXV, 1947.

Jones, E. 'Settlement Patterns in the Middle Teifi Valley', *Geography*, XXX, 1945.

Jones, E. 'Tregaron—A Welsh Market Town', *Geography*, XXXV, 1950.

Jones, E. 'Some Aspects of the Study of Settlement in Britain', *The Advancement of Science*, III, 1951.

Jones, G. R. J. 'Basic Patterns of Rural Settlemen in North Wales', *Trans. and Papers of Inst. of British Geographers*, No. 19, 1953.

Jones-Pierce, T. 'Medieval Settlement in Anglesey', *Trans. Anglesey Ant. Soc. and Field Club*, 1951.

MacNeill, E. 'The Native Place of St. Patrick', *Proc. Royal Irish Academy*, XXXVII, 1924-27.

Miller, A. A. 'The Entrenched Meanders of the Herefordshire Wye', *Geographical Journal*, LXXXV, 1935.

Miller, A. A. 'The 600 ft. Platform in Pembrokeshire and Carmarthenshire', *Geographical Journal*, XC, 1937.

Myres, J. N. L. 'Britain in the Dark Ages', *Antiquity*, IX, 1935.

Nash-Williams, V. E. 'Further Excavations at Caerwent, Monmouthshire 1923-5', *Archaeologia*, LXXX, 1930.

Nash-Williams, V. E. 'An Early Iron Age Hill-Fort at Llanmelin, near Caerwent, Monmouthshire', *Archaeologia Cambrensis*, LXXXVIII, 1933.

Nash-Williams, V. E. 'Excavations at Llantwit Major, Glamorgan, 1937', *Archaeologia Cambrensis*, XCII, 1937.

Nash-Williams, V. E. 'Some Dated Monuments of the "Dark Ages" in Wales', *Archaeologia Cambrensis*, XCIII, 1938.

Nash-Williams, V. E. 'Excavation of the Roman Villa at Llantwit Major, Glamorgan, 1938', *Archaeologia Cambrensis*, XCIII, 1938.

Nash-Williams, V. E. 'An Early Iron Age Coastal Camp at Sudbrook, Monmouthshire', *Archaeologia Cambrensis*, XCIV, 1939.

Palmer, A. E. 'Notes on the Early History of Bangor-is-coed', *Y Cymmrodor*, X, 1889.

Phillips, C. W. 'Excavation of a Hut Group at Pant-y-Saer, Anglesey', *Archaeologia Cambrensis*, LXXXIX, 1934.

Power, P. 'The Bounds and Extents of Irish Parishes', *Feilscribhinn Torna*, Cork University Press, 1947.

Prothero, R. M. 'Bristol Channel Coastlands : Early Cultural Contacts', *Scottish Geographical Magazine*, Vol. 65, 1949.

Radford, C. A. Ralegh, 'Tintagel : The Castle and Celtic Monastery', *Antiquaries Journal*, XV, 1935.

Randall, H. J. 'Roman Period' in *A Hundred Years of Welsh Archaeology*, Cambrian Archaeological Association, 1846-1946.

Richards, R. 'Ardudwy and its Ancient Churches' in *Harlech Studies*, Cardiff, 1938.

Richards, R. and Lloyd, R. G. 'The Old Church of Llandanwg', *Archaeologia Cambrensis*, XC, 1935.

Rodger, J. W. 'Llantwit Major, Glamorgan, Excavations', *Archaeologia Cambrensis*, XV, 1915.

Savory, H. N. 'List of Hill-Forts and other Earthworks in Wales', I. Glamorgan. *Bull. Board of Celtic Studies*, XIII, Pt. III, 1949.

Scott, Sir Lindsay. 'Gallo-British Colonies', *Proceedings Prehistoric Society*, XIV, 1948.

Stallybrass, B. 'Recent Discoveries at Clynnogfawr', *Archaeologia Cambrensis*, XIV, 1914.

Stenton, Sir F. M. 'The Historical Bearing of Place-Name Studies : England in the Sixth Century', *Trans. Royal Historical Soc.* (Series 4), XXI, 1939.

Stevens, C. E. 'Magnus Maximus in British History', *Etudes Celtiques*, III, 1938.

Stevens, C. E. 'Gildas Sapiens', *The English Historical Review*, Vol. 56, 1941.

Sylvester, D. 'The Hill-Villages of England and Wales', *Geographical Journal*, CX, 1947.

Sylvester, D. 'Rural Settlement in Anglesey', *Trans. Anglesey Antiquarian Soc. and Field Club*, 1949.

Wade-Evans, A. W. 'Beuno Sant', *Archaeologia Cambrensis*, LXXXV, 1930.

Watson, W. J. 'The Cult of St. Cadoc in Scotland', *Scottish Gaelic Studies*, II, 1927.

Wheeler, R. E. M. 'Roman and Native in Wales : an Imperial Frontier Problem', *Y Cymmrodor*, XXXI, 1921.

Williams, H. 'The Christian Church in Wales', *Trans. Hon. Soc. Cymmrodorion* 1893-4.

Williams, Sir Ifor, 'When did British become Welsh?', *Trans. Anglesey Antiquarian Soc. and Field Club*, 1939.

Williams, Sir Ifor. 'Hen Chwedlau', *Trans. Hon. Soc. Cymmrodorion*, 1946-47.

Williams, Sir Ifor. 'Wales and the North', *Trans. Cumb. and Westmorland Ant. and Arch. Soc.*, Vol. LI, (New Series), 1952.

M

INDEX